"The home should be the treasure chest of living."
– Le Corbusier

Susan Redman

CURATED LIVING

Elegant Interiors and Artful Homes

images
Publishing

CONTENTS

Introduction	7
Art House | Australia	8
Belgravia Townhouse | United Kingdom	20
Brahegatan Apartment | Sweden	34
Carlotta Take Two Residence | Australia	44
Light House | Australia	60
Marylebone Pied-à-Terre | United Kingdom	76
Matchpoint House | Australia	90
Moore Park Residence | Canada	106
Napa Valley House | United States	122
New School Residence | The Netherlands	142
Pacific Palisades Residence | United States	156
Place Dauphine Pied-à-Terre | France	174
Queen's Park Terrace | United Kingdom	188
Shady Canyon Residence | United States	202
State Street Townhouse | United States	220
Stockholm Residence | Sweden	238
Subdued Sophistication Condominium | Canada	252
Toxteth Terrace | Australia	266
The Homes and their Designers	282
About the Author	286

This book is dedicated to my family, who make our home a true sanctuary, filled with love and inspiration.

INTRODUCTION

In today's fast-paced world, the desire for tranquillity at home has ignited a new wave of interior design focused on softness, comfort and a visual sensibility. *Curated Living: Elegant Interiors and Artful Homes* explores this trend in residential design across Europe, North America and Australia.

The book features sophisticated, art-filled homes that serve as sanctuaries from the outside world. Each of the 18 chapters focuses on a unique residence. Many are sensitively renovated heritage houses—Victorian terraces, Edwardian mansions, brownstones and historic city apartments—where old-world elegance coexists with contemporary updates. Others are sprawling properties, fully transformed while retaining subtle nods to their original Spanish colonial, Italianate or minimalist styles.

Despite their varied origins, these homes share a commitment to serenity and refinement. Natural materials such as veined marble and grooved timber abound, often shaped or moulded into organic forms. Neutral, pale and smoky palettes dominate, while umbers and charcoals, along with occasional pops of saturated colour, add depth and character to the captivating interiors.

The decor and furnishings are spare yet intentional, subtle yet inviting, imbuing each space with understated luxury. Textured upholstery, sheer drapes and crafted linens offer tactile delight, while rounded furniture creates visual harmony. Whimsical collections and thought-provoking artwork and sculptures spark joy and intrigue. Every element, carefully curated and arranged, tells a story of comfort, grace and quiet sophistication.

The true stars of this book, however, are the interior designers and architectural visionaries whose creativity and ingenuity breathe new life into these spaces. Each has been interviewed about the concepts and processes they engaged to transform these homes. Their narratives are illustrated by atmospheric, intimate imagery captured by some of the world's leading photographers of award-winning residential design.

Through evocative photography and the insights of exceptionally talented designers, the beautiful interiors detailed in *Curated Living* come to life, inviting you to linger, dream and find inspiration to create your own artful sanctuary at home.

– Susan Redman

I acknowledge the First Nations peoples of the lands on which the homes in this book are built. I also pay my respects to the Gadigal and Wangal people of the Eora Nation in Australia, the traditional custodians of the land on which I live and work.

Bayside, Melbourne, Australia

ART HOUSE

Design studio Chelsea Hing
Photography Rhiannon Taylor

"I believe our houses are a stage for living, for creating joy and connection. It's no small thing to design spaces that uplift and delight us, but also bring ease."
– Chelsea Hing

This heritage-protected, two-storey Victorian-era home on a Melbourne inner-city block presented designer Chelsea Hing with an opportunity to address the spatial challenges typical of terrace houses. There wasn't enough room for the new owners, a professional couple with two children, and the layout was confusing despite having been previously renovated. On the plus side, the property benefited from being a stone's throw from the beach in a leafy bayside suburb, offering the family a prime location.

Chelsea sought to update and extend the home where possible to overcome prior design compromises. "The scope of works increased to encompass most of the house," says Chelsea, who collaborated with draftsman Mat Elkan. The clunky living room was reorganised, interiors refreshed with new fixtures and fittings and the rear kitchen, pantry and laundry were demolished to increase the footprint.

"The only additional space we could gain was in the small rear section of the ground floor, where we extended to the boundary to expand the laundry and create space for a new pantry," explains Chelsea. "Upstairs, we crafted a primary suite by converting an adjacent bedroom into a new walk-in wardrobe and ensuite, relocating the third bedroom to the rear with a central bath and a rumpus overlooking the courtyard."

Elsewhere, Chelsea's approach was to retain the existing footprint and make adjustments with the most impact on volume, space and flow. After updating the functional zones, the team capitalised on the home's charm and orientation. "As the end terrace in a run of eight, the corner block location was a significant asset in terms of natural light and aspect, a rare advantage in terrace houses," says Chelsea.

Aesthetically, Chelsea's plan was to balance the old-world charm of the terrace's original details with the modern confidence of bold accents. To that end, the interiors received a contemporary edge with new steel-framed doors and windows strategically installed, including a beautiful arched window in the primary bedroom. "Retaining the classical elements of the home while adding contemporary ones was a wonderful undertaking," explains Chelsea.

Another challenge the design team faced was dealing with architectural elements that had reached the end of their lives, such as floors that had been sanded back one too many times. "As a designer, you want to honour the client's wishes to retain certain things, but as a professional, you also know the limitations," Chelsea notes. Despite these hurdles, the floors and other worn-out features were repaired or replaced, resulting in a strengthened and beautifully crafted home.

The heart of this transformation lies in the living room, a space that Chelsea describes as her favourite. "It's filled with light and art," she says. Here, and elsewhere on the ground level, the material palette is built around classic fundamentals: oak, black steel, mouldings and white walls, with an injection of colour and interest via the emerald-green kitchen tiles and other boldly coloured decor. "Furniture and art build on the materials to create three-dimensional depth in the palette," says Chelsea.

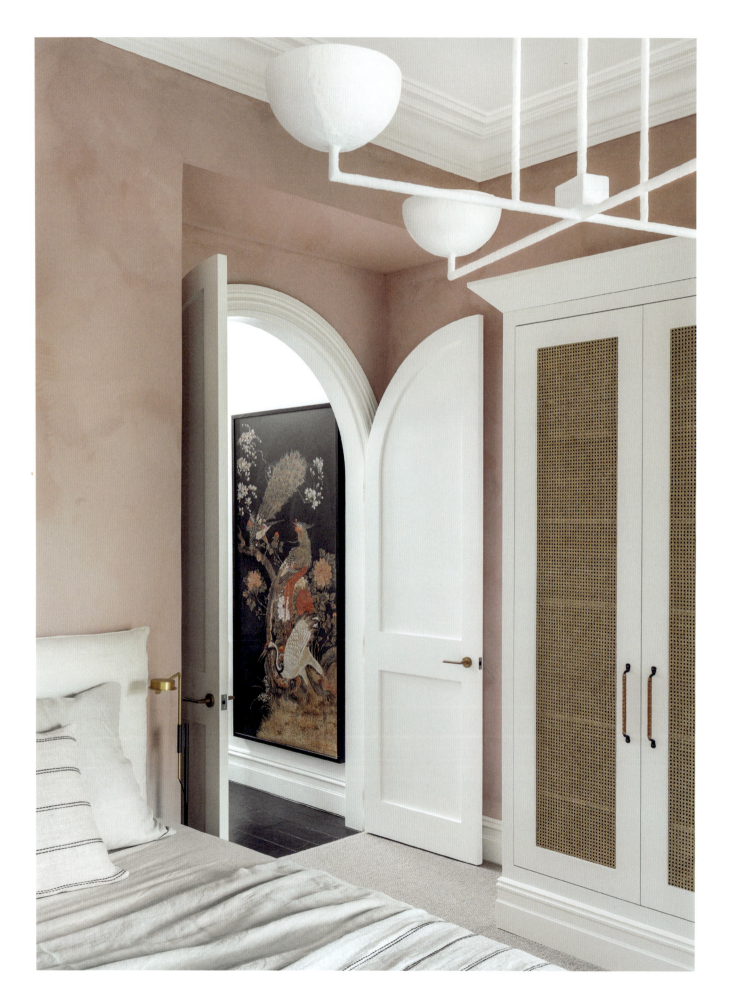

Upstairs, the design focuses on drawing out the colours of the primary suite, especially the mix of soft pinks and greens in the curtains. "We repeated these colours in the ensuite tiling, and matched similar oak tones in the joinery and rattan detailing to connect it to the ground-floor palette," Chelsea explains.

One of the exceptional features of this renovation is the decor, furniture and artwork curation, which encourages a sense of both comfort and delight. "We wanted to do some unorthodox things, especially in the communal spaces, such as hanging boundary-pushing art like the tapestry by Benjamin Barretto and the photographic artwork *Venus* by Petrina Hicks," says Chelsea. "The clients had an impressive art collection with pieces that were marked by memories of personal milestones or anniversaries. Our touch is really in how we hung the pieces in more unexpected ways, which has ultimately created a new feel throughout the space," Chelsea explains.

"We also layered the spaces with small sculptures, and brought in bold pattern, such as Sarah Ellison's striped Valentina screen." In furniture, Chelsea sourced classics such as the Le Bambole sofa by Mario Bellini, and new pieces like the Puffy Lounge Chair by Faye Toogood and HEM, and the Marenco sofa.

The contrast between old and new, upstairs and downstairs, and communal and private spaces proved to be the most appropriate way to honour the home's heritage while infusing it with a modern perspective. "The ground-floor rooms boast a dominant mix of avant-garde art and modern pieces while first-floor spaces exude a poetic romanticism," Chelsea describes. "For example, the primary bedroom's feminine wall treatment and textiles contrast with the kitchen's sleek, glossy, spearmint-toned tiles, rich Predia marble and midnight-black stone with caramel veining."

For Chelsea, designing a thoughtfully curated and artful home means creating a place to exhale, where people can truly be themselves. "I believe our houses are a stage for living, for creating joy and connection. It's no small thing to design spaces that uplift and delight us, but also bring ease. It's where we dream of what's possible," she says.

The owners' sentiments echo this philosophy. "Chelsea designed a beautiful, liveable space that responded to our art collection, but most importantly, felt like our home. Her vision reflected our taste and our love of art and brought these together with elegant simplicity and a cohesion that make this a lovely space to live. Her eye for detail and visual elements balanced well with her practicality to solve design issues."

Ultimately, this artistically crafted renovation by Chelsea Hing and her team not only addressed the spatial constraints and design challenges but also transformed the terrace into a sanctuary of art, family and home.

Belgravia, London, United Kingdom

BELGRAVIA TOWNHOUSE

Design studio State of Craft
Photography Nick Rochowski

"A good home interior should be akin to a reliable friend who can raise your spirits, offer a warm embrace and embody honesty and authenticity."
– Daniel Goldberg

This six-storey Georgian townhouse stands reborn in the heart of Belgravia, part of the prestigious Grosvenor Estate developed in the 19th century and renowned for its parks and grand architecture. The elegant residence, complete with a connected mews building, serves as a sanctuary of calm and tranquillity for a discerning art-collecting couple and their grown-up children.

At the time of purchase, the townhouse suffered from outdated interiors and services, which was in stark contrast to the attractive, manicured public garden square it overlooks. To modernise the home while honouring its heritage, the interior renovation was entrusted to London-based international design firm State of Craft. "Our client wanted to restore and adapt this historic townhouse to provide them with a place to stay for their frequent visits to London," explains Daniel Goldberg, founder and director of State of Craft. "There was a dual requirement to create a relaxing and comfortable family retreat, while offering a wonderful place for hosting dinner parties and accommodating guests."

Pringle Richards Sharratt Architects was commissioned to restore the main house and redesign the mews building. "This new addition incorporates a media room, gym and a luminous family kitchen space adjacent to a private courtyard," says Daniel. "The kitchen serves as a contemporary heart to a restored and revitalised heritage property."

State of Craft worked closely with the architects on the design and development of all aspects of the interiors, including the layouts and the integration of structure and services. "Our scope extended to the fit-out design of all areas, including living rooms, five bedrooms and six bathrooms, selection of all furniture, and the curation of artwork in collaboration with Richeldis Fine Arts," says Daniel. The project team also worked with George Sexton Associates on the lighting design.

One of the most significant challenges the designers faced was respecting the heritage-listed status of the building while introducing contemporary elements. "We collaborated with the planning department of the local council to uncover the original fabric of the interiors," Daniel explains. "This involved peeling back layers of 20th-century alterations to reveal the original Georgian architecture—a meticulous process that required several rounds of detailed design presentations to ensure a respectful integration of modern features."

According to Daniel, designing in a heritage context requires constant value judgments regarding what to restore and what to replace. "Our general approach was to clearly express new interventions and let those be set against heritage elements," he says. "For example, most of the features in the central staircase, including balustrades, treads and panelling, were original and could be saved or restored, whereas mantelpieces were typically lost and required a more differentiated approach where reinstated."

The final design aesthetic successfully harmonises the home's heritage character within a tranquil environment. Tall, elegant windows within white, formal stucco façades enhance the views of the iconic garden square outside and provide ample light for the front interior spaces. Generous glazing onto the internal courtyard and rear garden, along with additional skylights, permits natural sunlight into other areas of the home.

"London's garden squares, like the one this townhouse overlooks, are among England's most distinctive contributions to town planning," says Daniel. "Their verdant nature represents the classical ideal of *rus in urbe* or country in the city, where pockets of calm tranquillity are found amid the noise and traffic of a vibrant city."

This serene setting also inspired a restrained palette of colours, materials and textures throughout the home. "A muted palette of soft, earthy tones serves as a subtle backdrop to the art, light and life within the house," says Daniel. "We also chose a limited palette of material finishes to create a sense of generosity and continuity."

This consistency is achieved through a thoughtful selection of natural materials, such as honed limestone, wide-plank European oak flooring and clay-plastered walls with a set sheen. "We used solid, honest materials and different textures to appeal to the sense of touch," says Daniel. "Many furniture pieces and built-in joinery elements were crafted by some of the finest English artisans, adding bespoke craftsmanship to the interiors."

While unobtrusive finishes allow striking artwork, furniture and views of the garden square to take centre stage, the considered selection of both functional and decorative pieces creates a sense of comfort and delight. "The project provided us with the opportunity to curate an art collection from the outset," Daniel explains. "This seamless integration of artwork, built-in finishes and loose furniture embodies the Bauhaus tradition of a *Gesamtkunstwerk*, or total work of art, resulting in a timeless home that blends modern and historical elements with ease."

Throughout the home, a fluid conversation between the classical and contemporary plays out in a unique collection of artworks and objects, due in large part to the creative vision of savvy homeowners who have a flair for collecting antiques, bespoke European design and contemporary art, particularly British modernism. The property features major works by Richard Serra and Ben Nicholson as well as contemporary pieces by leading international and emerging artists Joaquim Chancho, Lawrence Calver, Terri Brooks, Alexi Tsioris and Gerry Judah.

Daniel is particularly proud of how Belgravia Townhouse bridges the formal grandeur of a 19th-century Georgian house with the warmth and functionality of a 21st-century home. "The home strikes a pleasing balance between spaces that are tranquil yet uplifting," he says. "A good home interior should be akin to a reliable friend who can raise your spirits, offer a warm embrace and embody honesty and authenticity."

Östermalm, Stockholm, Sweden

BRAHEGATAN APARTMENT

Design studio Liljencrantz Design
Photography Erik Lefvander

"As a designer, you fall in love with materials and objects and always have the drive to create something with them. That drive never stops, but you must know how to stop when it's perfect."
– Louise Liljencrantz

Renowned for her refined sense of style, Swedish designer Louise Liljencrantz created a haven of sophistication for her family's Stockholm apartment by layering material textures, leaning into a neutral colour palette and furnishing it with classic pieces, including her own designs. The spacious home, spanning nearly 200 square metres, is located in an 1883 apartment building on the stylish street of Brahegatan in upscale Östermalm, a district well known for its concentration of cafés, restaurants, museums and cultural spaces.

"I live here with my husband, two daughters, a dog and two cats," says Louise. "When we moved in, the apartment had six layers of old wallpaper and damaged floors, and it had not been renovated for at least 40 years. However, it was beautiful, with almost everything in its original state. Even so, it took about a year to renovate."

The apartment now has three large bedrooms, two bathrooms, a compact kitchen, dining room, living room and an office. A dressing room has been rebuilt with Louise's 'Palazzo' cabinetry that she recently designed for kitchen and bathroom company Kvänum. The new layout of the apartment allows for communal gatherings and private retreats, perfectly catering to the needs of a modern family.

As a testament to Louise's design philosophy, which blends modern elegance with timeless charm, she retained many of the apartment's original architectural features, including the Victorian cornices, wooden herringbone parquetry flooring, high ceilings and large windows. "The apartment faces southwest, making the direction of the sun crucial," says Louise. "The light and shadows that change with the movement of the sun bring a room to life. Our home is a wonderful light-filled place—it really has a soul."

With generous proportions and flooded with natural light, the home feels spacious without being overly formal. The magic of good design, Louise explains, is to smoothly integrate the visual poetry of the rooms by maintaining a consistent colour palette throughout. "I aimed for a fresh and light feel, like a day breeze," she says. "After experimenting with paint and colour combinations for a long time, I found the perfect recipe. The apartment is rendered in whites, shades of soft grey, green and beige, all pulled together with splashes of black and darker wood. This crisp, clean palette allows the details of the furniture and artworks to stand out."

This neutral palette creates a serene backdrop for Louise's impeccable furniture design choices. In the living room, a vintage Alanda coffee table designed by Paolo Piva takes central position, flanked by two charming mid-century wooden stools: the higher Tabouret Méribel and the lower Tabouret Berger, both designed by Charlotte Perriand and produced by Cassina.

Against the wall, a custom-made upholstered bench seat, with a design also inspired by Perriand, sits beneath a graphic black-and-white artwork by Finnish artist Jarmo Kurki. These pieces, alongside the fur-covered Botolo chair by Cini Boeri and two angular reupholstered antique lounge chairs by Walter Knoll, create a living space that is stylish, modern and inviting.

In the adjacent dining room, Louise's curated collection of furniture, lighting and artwork adds further sophistication. The Three-Arm Ceiling Lamp designed by Serge Mouille in the 1950s hangs over the table, which is surrounded by six Point chairs designed by Jonas Bohlin, providing a smart setting for family meals and gatherings. On the wall are two artworks by French artist Julian Arnaud.

Elsewhere, the home's classic bones are balanced with eye-catching elements like the slate-grey stone fireplace and wooden parquetry floors, creating an interflow between old and new. Louise sometimes uses the home to consider how her furniture designs for Veermakers, in prototype or in production, may work in situ. Her custom-designed pieces also add a personal touch to the decor.

Louise's love for rich textures and carefully chosen pieces is evident throughout her home, with luxurious soft furnishings enhancing every space. Yet it is in the misty-grey and snow-white primary bedroom where her talent for imbuing a space with serenity is best expressed. A velvet-upholstered bench and other textured elements add to the room's luxurious yet relaxed ambience. Overhead, a vintage Sputnik chandelier is suspended from the elaborate ceiling rose. "I particularly love the brass, velvet and linen of the bedroom as well as the ornate details," says Louise. "It's a relaxed yet stylish space to wake up in."

Every design detail has been considered in Louise's stylish city apartment, creating a home that is effortlessly chic and deeply personal. The home not only provides a warm and welcoming sanctuary for her family but proves that truly thoughtful design can transcend the trends of here and now. Louise's brand of timeless modernity is a guide for all, and is still current a decade on.

"I designed this apartment's interior almost 10 years ago, and it still looks the same," she says. "I've only changed the coffee table to one of my own designs and the sofa to match the table. I have also added some new art. Everything has its perfect spot, and it felt right from the beginning, allowing me more time to channel my creativity into my clients' projects. As a designer, you fall in love with materials and objects and always have the drive to create something with them. That drive never stops, but you must know how to stop when it's perfect."

Double Bay, Sydney, Australia

CARLOTTA TAKE TWO RESIDENCE

Design studio Esoteriko
Photography Dave Wheeler

"By layering textures and incorporating both old and new decor, we achieved a harmonious balance that highlights the architectural features while creating a welcoming atmosphere."
– Anna Trefely

Tasked with transforming the interiors of a sleek modern home for a second time, designer Anna Trefely faced the challenge of re-envisioning familiar spaces with a fresh, softer perspective. The result is Carlotta Take Two, a sophisticated home presenting a marriage of contemporary design and serene living, blending comfort, intimacy and elegance within its original robust architectural framework.

"The brief from the new owners, a professional couple with teenage and grown-up children, was to lighten and soften the contemporary concrete and steel bunker-like structure via a light touch of interior elements that provided comfort," explains Anna, principal of boutique design practice Esoteriko. "The design we devised responds to the way in which the family wanted to inhabit the space, allowing for both singular moments of retreat and hospitable group experiences."

Carlotta Take Two is a five-storey contemporary residence sited on a steep slope in the prestigious harbour-side suburb of Double Bay in Sydney. It has views across a leafy gully and spans approximately 500 square metres internally, with five bedrooms and six bathrooms spread across its steeply terraced levels. The open-plan layout creates a flowing connection between the interiors and the surrounding rooftops and treetops, bringing the area's natural beauty into focus from many of the rooms. Soaring full-height windows engage directly with the sky, offering breathtaking views that complement the interior palette.

The quandary Anna faced was significant: how to balance the masculine concrete and steel brutalist building with an interior design favouring a soft-edged, feminine quality without feeling contrived. "The clients' previous home was a light, bright terrace with a fresh white Hamptons flavour," says the designer. "It was a challenge to ensure that the particular freshness of their previous home could be translated and adapted into something appropriate in this architectural context, characterised as it was by a cool industrial edge."

A dedication to invention and an ability to push boundaries in design was key to Anna's approach. "Problem-solving is my great love," she says. "I'm a dog with a bone. I want to get more out of less."

Anna's solution was to layer soft furnishings, creating intimate settings within the larger rooms and defining spaces with floor coverings, such as the wool rugs in the living area and in the bedrooms, all custom-designed by Esoteriko. "We added light-washed timber joinery with bull-nosed edges, and tactile curves in furniture to further soften the angular forms of the architecture," she says. "The considered positioning of these shapes, combined with the extraordinary vistas visible from the interior, allowed us to create a space that felt poetic, polished and relaxed, perfectly suited to the new occupants' lifestyle."

One of the stand-out features of the residence is the open-plan living, dining and kitchen space, which occupies a full level of the house and opens out to a balcony overlooking the treetops. "This space has a strong emphasis on materiality and texture," notes Anna. "It is confidently layered with new joinery items, lighting and furnishings to reflect a mix of genres and forms."

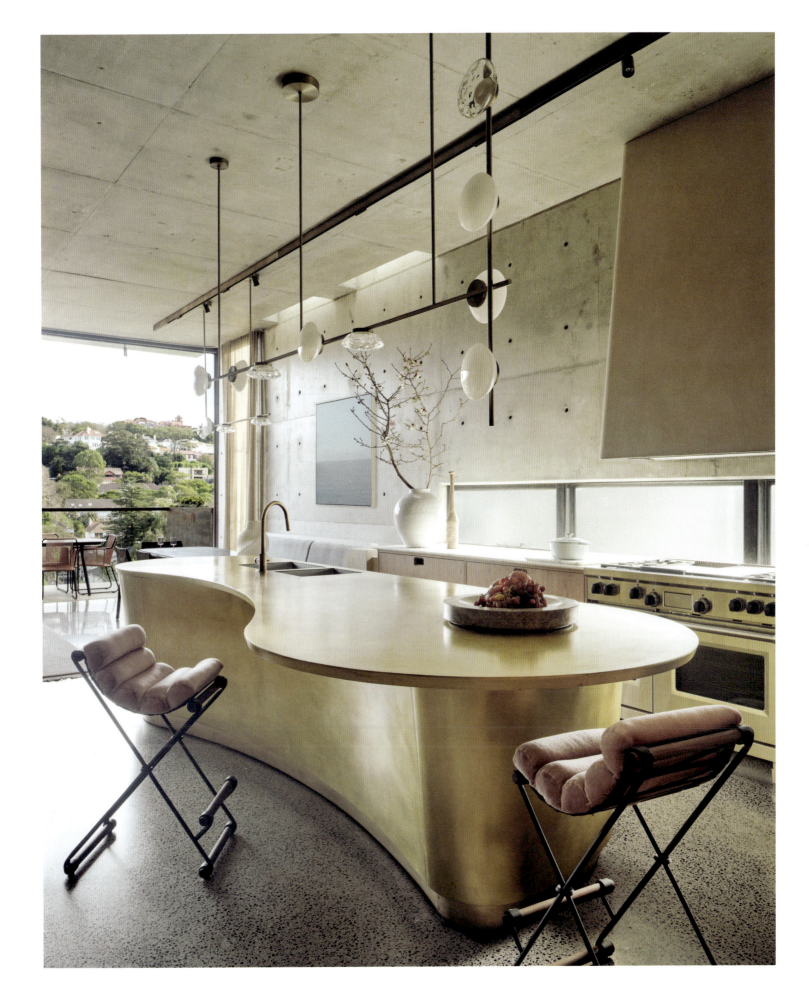

The kitchen itself is a marvel of design, with a raw brass-clad kidney-shaped island that serves as the heart of the home. "The sinuous curves of this sculptural piece facilitate flow and playfully test the edges of the kitchen," says Anna. "At over 4 metres long, it combines functions of preparation, dining, servery and workspace. With a renewed golden brass finish, the object acts like a warm internal sun, reflecting light from all angles during the day, and from a customised Ross Gardam pendant at night."

Colour plays a crucial role in the redesign of the interiors, serving as a counterpoint to the masculine elements of the raw off-form concrete walls and soffit, and black steel-framed fenestration. "We introduced flashes of blue and an array of pink hues to punctuate the areas, such as artworks with pink highlights in both living spaces," says Anna. In the casual lounge room downstairs hangs work by Yvonne Robert, while *Grasshopper* by Ben Crase is in the open-plan living area. A painting titled *Blue Sea 2* by Chris Langlois hangs over the grey banquette and table in the dining area on the same level. These colours add warmth and intimacy to the space, creating a harmonious balance between the masculine and feminine elements.

Furniture selection was crucial to achieving a sense of comfort and delight in the home's interior. "Our directive was to provide conversational and comfortable settings, as well as new and adapted joinery and decorative elements within the existing space," says Anna. "We aimed to balance the boldness of the concrete structure with a sense of lightness, ensuring the interior scale was appropriate and infused with a sense of fun."

For this purpose, Anna chose playful, modern furniture such as the pink-velvet vintage Djinn chaise longue by Olivier Mourgue for Airborne, a cream curved sofa by Christophe Delcourt, an oval coffee table custom-made by Australian studio idéék and blue-velvet Utrecht armchairs for the living room. These are anchored by a luxurious rug and complemented by a custom joinery wall unit in blonde timber on a curved white Calacatta marble foundation. Elsewhere, refurbished classic vintage pieces sit alongside custom-designed items, both locally and globally sourced.

In the bedrooms, Anna left the concrete walls as backdrops to counterpoint the warmly textured environments. "We chose refined pale colourings and materiality, which you immediately see in the headboards upholstered in soft custom coverings and in the curved cabinetry crafted from beautifully grained warm oak."

Through thoughtful planning and curated decor in the revision of Carlotta Take Two, the Esoteriko team has delivered a calming sanctuary for living. What Anna loves most about the finished design is how the interiors reflect the comfort and sophistication expected from the owners' original brief. "There is a delicate softness interspersed with punchy elements that comfortably sit against its cool industrial backdrop," she says.

Vaucluse, Sydney, Australia

LIGHT HOUSE

Design studio Smac Studio
Photography Dave Wheeler

"While the house is classic, the furnishings and decor are contemporary, which creates complexity."
– Shona McElroy

Directly across the road from the historic Macquarie Lighthouse on the dramatic Pacific Ocean coastline in exclusive Vaucluse, Sydney, is a grand residence that recently underwent a comprehensive renovation by interior designer Shona McElroy, founder of Smac Studio. The transformation of the home into a bright, airy residence, now aptly named Light House, was both challenging and rewarding.

Originally built as an Italianate-style villa in 1989, the house had a neoclassical layout with distinct formal and informal living areas. The new owners, however, desired a functional and stylish open-plan design that seamlessly connected indoor and outdoor spaces, ideal for entertaining.

"The brief was to create bright, open spaces that flow out to the pool and pergola, with a broad aim to meld the classic with the contemporary, embracing the existing architecture's Italianate style while future-proofing it for modern living. We wanted to ensure that the entire home felt timeless," says Shona.

One of the most significant challenges for the studio was the tight timeline: just three months for design and nine months for construction. "We had trouble with lead times for certain items, so things were changing on the fly, but the home still has all the elements I wanted from the beginning," Shona says.

Despite the rushed schedule, the design team was determined not to compromise on character and quality. "We always wanted certain features, such as curved forms, a journey from formal to informal, the marble checkerboard floor and the artful lighting. Even though the build time was short, we didn't skimp on character."

The result is a home Shona describes as "neutral but layered with themes of classicism and modernity intertwined". She particularly loves the timelessness of the finished design, comparing it to "a little black dress with a pearl necklace—something that will be current for a long time". This quality allows the home's aesthetic to evolve with any future changes in decor without losing its core elegance.

Key to achieving the cohesive look was the selection of materials, particularly the grey-and-white marble used throughout the house. "Arabescato is an elegant Italian stone with dramatic textured veining," Shona says. "This is quite a big house by Sydney's Eastern Suburbs standards, 345 square metres, so to use the Arabescato repeatedly keeps the design consistent and links the spaces."

The colour palette was another critical aspect of the design. The clients opted for a warm, neutral palette that would accommodate future changes in furniture styles. "We achieved that using warm timbers, Arabescato marble and detailed wall panelling," Shona explains.

A thoughtful combination of modern furniture, soft furnishings and contemporary art created a playful yet sophisticated atmosphere. "While the house is classic, the furnishings and decor are contemporary, which creates complexity," says Shona.

Statement seating includes the voluptuous Sedia lounge chair from Dimitri Vargas and the Poppy Pouf from Fred International in the cigar room, and the playful Wiggle Side Chair and Sequoia Pouf at the dining table. These chairs offer warmth and texture, while still life, figurative and abstract artworks, such as *Lola and Frutus* by Lauren Jones, *Nude* by Samuel Condon and *Illusive Travelers ll* by Mandy Francis, provide detail, colour and a sense of drama to the rooms.

One of the gracious home's stand-out architectural features greets visitors at the entrance. The staircase, originally displaying harsh lines formed by an iron railing and balusters, has been softened by a sculptural moulding of curvaceous white Venetian plaster. Shona emphasised the loftiness of the existing double-height foyer with a chandelier and generous skylight, anchoring this with a checkerboard-patterned floor featuring Verde Alpi and Carrara marble.

This nod to grandeur enhances the entrance and sets the tone for the rest of the home. "There's a real sense of arrival," says Shona. "You enter into this light, airy, double-height space with the Cloud chandelier above you, passing the sweeping plaster curves of the staircase."

Smac Studio carefully zoned the journey through the home. "I love all the different layers, materials and shifts of light as you move from one room to the next," Shona says. "From the entry, you walk across the checkerboard floor passing by two facing marble-framed portals leading to either a formal dining room on the right or a moody cigar room on the left. Parquetry oak flooring then ushers you into the bright, open-plan modern kitchen and informal living spaces at the rear." To contrast with the predominance of white walls, the same moody character of the cigar room is repeated in the study, which is located off the entrance foyer.

Upstairs, there are four bedrooms, including the large primary bedroom where beige window curtains and a richly coloured tapestry bedcover adds softness. Three of the bedrooms share two bathrooms while the spacious primary bedroom features an ensuite bathroom and a luxurious his-and-hers walk-in wardrobe with two curved island benches topped in stone.

For Shona, designing a curated and artful home means creating spaces with subtle classicism, lots of curves and few hard edges. "Curvaceous elements are so much more embracing and cosy than rigid angles," she says, referencing the home's arches, linen curtains, curved balustrades and grooved edges on the kitchen island and fireplace.

Reflecting on her successful trajectory, Shona credits her background as a qualified architect and the creative freedom granted by early clients as pivotal moments. These experiences have allowed Shona to develop a flexible approach to interior design, showcased in the Light House project. "This house shows our versatility. We are known for our colour schemes, but we can also deliver more traditional, formal homes that still exhibit our love of modernity and a sense of daring."

Marylebone, London, United Kingdom

MARYLEBONE PIED-À-TERRE

Design studio Maddux Creative
Photography Michael Sinclair

"Luxurious materials and sumptuous fabrics in the living and bedroom areas, such as patterned cushions and textured curtains, provide a cohesive and elegant sensibility to the entire apartment."
– Jo leGleud

The vibrant central London borough of Marylebone features many fine homes from the Georgian, Victorian and Edwardian eras, as well as Art Deco–style properties from the 1920s. In one such building, a spacious apartment serves as a European pied-à-terre for a Los Angeles–based couple and their two daughters. It has been skilfully transformed by Maddux Creative, an interior design firm founded by Jo leGleud and Scott Maddux, with offices in London and New York.

"The Marylebone apartment allowed us to honour historical elements while injecting the space with contemporary design," says Scott. "The challenge was to respect its Art Deco origins while introducing modern touches that made the space feel current and lived-in."

To that end, Maddux Creative remodelled the two-bedroom apartment by merging British classicism and Parisian charm with modernity. Original features, such as mouldings, parquetry flooring and coffered ceilings, were retained and restored while functionality was updated. This provided the home with European sophistication akin to that found in Parisian Haussmann or Berliner Altbau apartments.

However, the designers were careful to quietly weave contemporary accents into the home's heritage bones. "We felt it was important to blur the line between being able to tell if something was original or new," Scott says. "This allowed us to push boundaries and flex our artistic ideas, an approach that was crucial in overcoming the biggest challenge: creating a space that felt both luxurious and liveable without resembling a gallery."

Throughout the apartment, tactile materials and styled vignettes dot the interior spaces, offering plenty of visual interest and referencing the dynamic and fashionable character of Marylebone. Elsewhere, pastel hues and refined wall treatments create a canvas for the owners' growing contemporary art collection, which includes works by artists Charles Gaines, Ross Chisholm and Silvina Der-Meguerditchian.

"Our goal was to establish a home that exuded relaxation and freshness, avoiding extremes of overpowering elements or blandness," Jo explains. "My training in embroidery honed my eye for a balanced integration of textures and colours, a theme reflected throughout the entire apartment."

With these design principles in mind, the Maddux Creative team employed a soft, muted palette of pale aqua and chalky off-white with accents of red and gold. "This was inspired by a desire to create a calming yet sophisticated atmosphere that complemented the homeowners' art collection," says Jo.

The apartment spans an elegantly designed space and features two bedrooms with ensuites, a powder room, a spacious entrance hallway, a kitchen, and a living room with a dining area that opens to a library.

The neat and compact burnished brass-clad kitchen makes an exceptionally strong statement. "We opted for a galley-style kitchen. It's small but perfectly formed," says Scott. "We chose slabs of Calacatta Verde marble for countertops and an injection of subtle colour, and painted the room in the delightfully edible hue of 'Sesame' from Paint Library London. This creates a lovely vignette visible through the open door."

The largest room, which contains both the sitting and dining areas, showcases a gradual transition of colour through layered shapes and shades over the existing wall panelling. Experimentation continues in the adjoining library, where three different shades of green highlight the mouldings. "The original elements provide a historical context, and are complemented by the contemporary, such as the colour-block paint effect and modern furnishings," Jo explains.

Decor for the residence is a mix of custom, contemporary and vintage items. The designers commissioned bespoke pieces for the apartment, notably the serpentine sofa in the living room, based on an antique design. Stand-out designer pieces are the Lampert + Harper daybed upholstered in red leather and the mirrored artwork by Sabine Marcelis and Brit van Nerven that hangs above the fireplace. Other designer furniture includes a vintage Eero Saarinen sofa, a contemporary Christophe Delcourt sofa, a mid-century Paolo Buffa armchair and a sleek Villiers cocktail table.

Turkish rugs, French antique furniture, Danish dining chairs, global textiles and international art reflect the homeowners' love of travel and culture. "Luxurious materials and sumptuous fabrics in the living and bedroom areas, such as patterned cushions and textured curtains, provide a cohesive, elegant sensibility to the entire apartment," says Jo. "For example, dark-blue textured wallpaper in the primary bedroom provides a soulful backdrop, allowing for a layering of textures in bed linens and furniture."

The soft-pink guest bedroom offers a fresh and subdued space for slumber and features a magical artwork by Lorna Simpson above the bed. The subtle pink theme carries into the ensuite, balanced with buttery-green accents.

The ensuite bathrooms are unified by intricate Jean Cocteau–inspired mosaic floors and polished plaster walls. The recurring curved arches evoke a feeling of 1920s glamour, intrinsic to the fabric of the building. "The bespoke metal shower screen we designed completes this stunning vignette and provides elegant function," says Jo. "We also commissioned Isabella Day to paint a playful mural inspired by French artist Christian Bérard for the powder room."

Set against a backdrop that fuses the old with the new, the smooth flow of soft muted shades punctuated by accents of red and gold creates an atmosphere that is glamorous and relaxing. "Every detail, from the carefully selected colour palette to the bespoke furniture, was aimed at creating an elegant and personal sanctuary for our clients," says Scott.

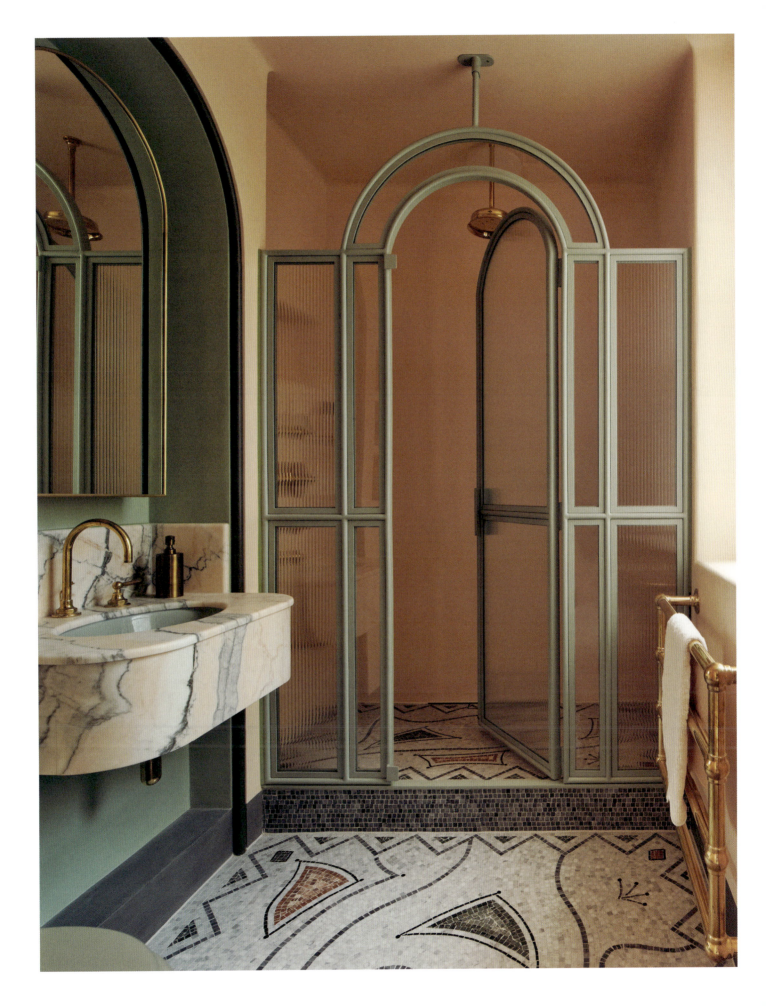

Strathfield, Sydney, Australia

MATCHPOINT HOUSE

Design studio Duet
Photography Anson Smart

"Their home aspirations were also unequivocally modern—luxurious and warm, colourful and playful—and they wanted each room to tell its own story."
– Duet

In Strathfield, an historic suburb of Sydney known for its stately homes, stands Matchpoint, a sprawling Tudor Revival residence built in 1916 and surrounded by manicured gardens, sweeping lawns and a tennis court. The owners were recommended Dominique Brammah and Shannon Shlom, founders of the interior design practice Duet. Quickly establishing a wonderful connection with the designer duo, they bounced around ideas and inspiration for the home's update before entrusting the pair with a great deal of creative freedom.

"The young family of six are avid travellers and they wanted a style of home inspired by their favourite hotels and resorts across Europe—a timeless home that nods to the many places they have stayed in and loved," says Dominique. The owners provided reference images from their travels. "These featured heavily detailed wall panelling, moulded ceilings and cornices, ornate joinery, deep skirtings and sinuous curves, combining the Belle Epoque era and manor-house traditions. Yet their home aspirations were also unequivocally modern—luxurious and warm, colourful and playful—and they wanted each room to tell its own story."

The challenge of resurrecting this historical gem into a magnificent two-storey home with five bedrooms, five bathrooms and newly built outdoor living areas, a pool and self-contained guesthouse was significant. "The home had been renovated over the years, however, the new owners were committed to elevating the interiors to a level befitting the history, original architecture and craftsmanship of the home," says Shannon. "Our task was to restore it to its former elegance, with beautiful finishes and exquisite detailing becoming of a stately yet robust contemporary family home."

The design aimed for a blending of historic architectural elements with a modern sensibility and contemporary utility. The original features, such as jewel-coloured leadlight windows, moulded ceilings, cornices and detailed panelling, were key to the design direction for the project. "We aimed to create a layered, timeless and energising family home. It made sense to take an artisanal approach in designing, selecting and curating the spaces."

One of the most significant interventions was moving the traditional straight staircase, which dominated the entry. "We replaced it with a sculpted, sweeping spiral staircase with Carrara marble treads, neatly dividing the floor plan into two zones: formal and casual," says Shannon. "This adjustment honoured the original proportions while creating a generous, open, contemporary space."

The selection and application of materials played a pivotal role in achieving the desired aesthetic. "The exemplary installation of custom-designed, European-oak parquetry flooring, custom marble flooring and an abundance of panelling, mouldings and arches are testament to the exceptional craftspeople who collaborated with us," says Dominique. The design also included bespoke furniture pieces, such as custom-made stone bedside tables, brass-spun bedside lights and crafted pendant lights.

The designers introduced tactile opulence through sophisticated furniture, mixing some of their own designs alongside iconic pieces. In the formal lounge, the designers' curved custom sofa, velvet ball cushions and rug perfectly complement the 1970 Etcetera lounge chair and foot stool by Jan Ekselius. In the family living room, a playful combination of elements includes a custom plinth topped with vintage Fabergé eggs, and an Esedra pouf from Poltrona Frau.

"We explored custom-designed furniture, furnishings and lighting for the home, as well as hunting worldwide for vintage pieces," says Shannon. "The lighting selection, in particular, is a worldly curation of many eras. A Stellar Grape floor light by Sebastian Herkner for Pulpo in the family living room speaks to the Drop System Chandelier by Lindsey Adelman over the dining table. In the primary ensuite, a vintage Barovier&Toso pendant light evokes the romance of another era."

While the home predominantly features traditional ornamentation, the contemporary twist offered by modern furniture is complemented by sympathetic soft furnishings. "We designed a lot of textured and upholstered elements including sofas, bedheads and carpets, including the checkered floor covering in the primary bedroom. We even had the clients' initials embroidered in raspberry red on bed linen," says Dominique. "Luxe finishes including velvets, durable leathers, marble and brass highlights abound, injecting warmth, light and life."

Colour palettes were carefully chosen to create distinct atmospheres within different areas of the home. "The formal living room is subdued and serene, softly coloured and sophisticated, contrasting with the deeper jewel-toned hues of the more relaxed, informal living areas," says Shannon. "For the kids' playroom, we ramped things up with colour and bold stripes on the ceiling, creating an energetic grandeur and profound sense of joy."

Set on a 2,036-square-metre property, and with an outdoor kitchen and fully equipped guesthouse, Matchpoint is of a scale well beyond most residential projects. "To have carte blanche to lean into whatever we dreamt up for the home was such a unique opportunity," says Dominique.

The end result brought immense satisfaction to everyone. "Seeing both the customisation and personalisation reflecting the owners' passions throughout the home gives us a great sense of achievement," says Shannon. A highlight is the custom stone floor in the games room, a labour of love that took many iterations to perfect. "It embodies the culmination of a beautifully fruitful and rewarding collaboration of ideas shared between us and our client."

As they reflect on the transformation of Matchpoint, the Duet designers emphasise the importance of creating spaces with emotional impact. "The entire property is designed for a family who loves entertaining, yet the spaces feel equally inviting and welcoming once the party is over," says Dominique. "Ultimately, each space is designed for its emotional impact, ensuring the home is a grand stage for social gatherings and a cosy retreat for family life."

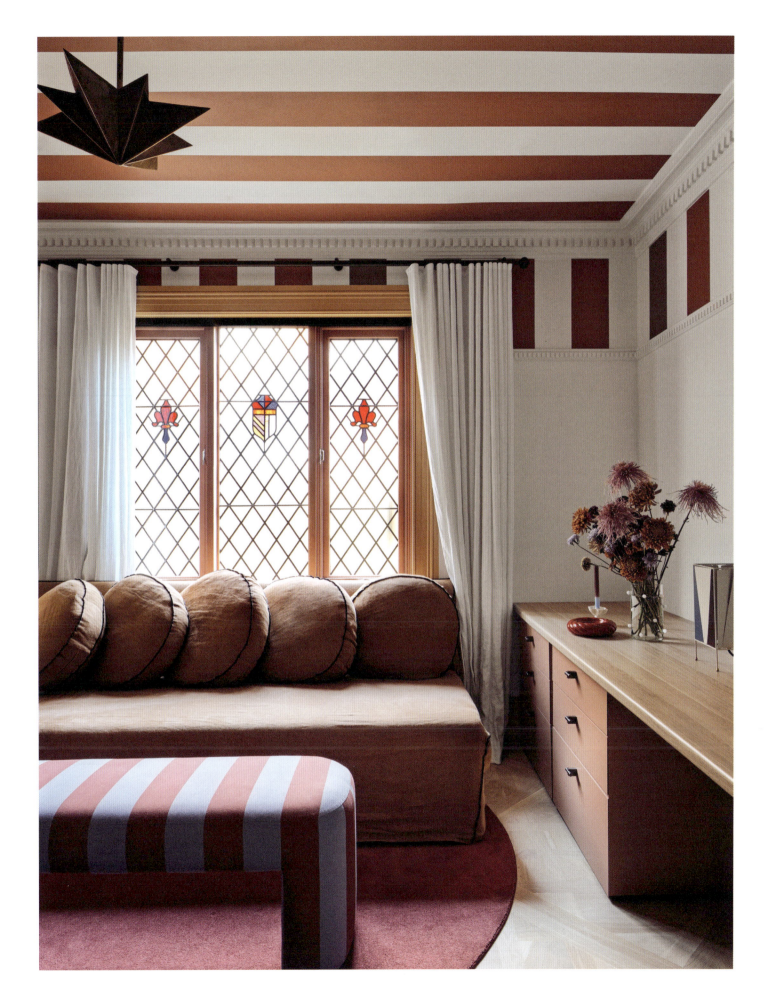

Rosedale, Toronto, Canada

MOORE PARK RESIDENCE

Design studio EM Design Studio
Photography Younes Bounhar of Double Space Photo

"The cornerstones of beauty are fundamental to our quest to seek perfection—the standard that we judge our work and dedication to our craft."
– Elizabeth Metcalfe

In Toronto's historic neighbourhood Rosedale, known for its lush tree-lined streets, winding trails, ancient ravines and some of the city's loveliest homes, stands Moore Park—a property that embodies elegance, sophistication and familial warmth. This distinctive home is a testament to the collaborative vision of its owners and the creative prowess of interior designer Elizabeth Metcalfe.

Elizabeth studied graphic design before moving into the world of interior design, later forming EM Design Studio. Her encounters within creative arts continue to inform her approach to home design today. "I am constantly seeking out moments of beauty that I translate into our studio's work," she says. "I'm naturally drawn to simplistic, fluid lines and shapes, whether they are on a Greek vase, a cut-out figure by Henri Matisse, a chalkboard painting by Cy Twombly or a sculpture carved by Henry Moore."

With a keen eye for composition, Elizabeth approached the redesign of Moore Park with a masterful blend of pragmatism and artistic flair. Her brief was simple and straightforward: to design a beautiful family home that reflected the unique style and fashionable point of view of her clients—a couple relocating from New York with their two young sons and three pets.

"Our challenge was to take a very dated layout and reinvent it," says Elizabeth. Originally built in the late 1980s, the home's new plan includes a substantial kitchen in which to cook and entertain friends, a spacious primary suite with his-and-hers walk-in wardrobes and a luxurious ensuite, and colourful bedrooms for the children. "My clients wanted the house to feel warm and modern, to incorporate natural, honest materials and to exhibit an overall feeling of ease and comfort," she says.

With meticulous attention to detail, Elizabeth crafted a narrative of space and light within Moore Park's sprawling 557 square metres spread across three storeys. "The main floor now features a living room and dining room flanked by a central staircase, with a kitchen and family room along the back of the house," explains Elizabeth. "The living room opens up to a sun-filled garden room overlooking a leafy ravine, and has a study ingeniously hidden behind a secret door. The second floor is divided into two main areas: the primary suite and a separate suite of rooms for the children. The third floor is a welcoming guest suite beautifully wrapped in a luxurious handpainted de Gournay wall covering."

A selection of the finest materials and natural finishes played a significant role in Elizabeth's renovation, from clay-based paints and blond oil-rubbed oak floorboards to artisanal plaster details and luxurious fabrics and textiles. This is particularly evident in the dramatic marble-encased primary ensuite—a space the designer regards as the 'star' of the home. "The bold veining of the marble is tempered by barley blush hand-dyed cashmere sheer curtains, a luxuriously soft alpaca hand-loomed area rug, humble oak flooring and a voluptuous pale green bathtub from The Water Monopoly," she says. "There is a palatable quietness in this room by a thoughtful interaction of objects, textures, silhouettes and colour."

Similarly, in the powder room, tucked between the kitchen and the study, a combination of juxtaposing materiality adds dimension, depth and visual interest. "Custom-coloured tiles designed by Sebastian Herkner are stacked vertically to balance the bleached oak horizontal banding that wraps around the room. A beautiful marble vanity is paired with polished nickel to add softness and lift to the graphic tile pattern," says Elizabeth.

While every corner of Moore Park bears the mark of Elizabeth's discerning eye for surface treatments, the designer's furniture choices elevate the levels of comfort and sophistication. The primary suite features handcrafted Sawkille Co. side tables, a restored Adrian Pearsall mid-century chair, an Apparatus Cloud chandelier and an Atelier Février rug.

Elsewhere, artisanal artefacts and vintage pieces pepper the scheme, tailoring the design to the homeowners' love of handmade crafts and collectible textiles. "Handmade pieces stand the test of time, fostering an emotional connection that enhances our daily lives. In a perfection-obsessed world, it's the slight imperfections that reveal an artisan's touch," Elizabeth says.

Guided by an intuitive understanding of hues and tones, the colour palette for Moore Park speaks to the soul, with a symphony of inky blacks, warming browns and soft, enveloping pinks. "Creating a colour palette requires a very careful hand," Elizabeth says. "It must never feel contrived, forced or formulative. Instead, the palette should feel intuitive, natural and fluid."

This can be seen in the cosy and inviting kitchen and breakfast area, where an intimate banquette table nestled in a hand-plastered dome was designed to convey a more casual feeling. "A curved mohair sofa provides a perfect spot for the family to gather and their large dog to lounge in the sun-filled room. There is also functional storage space with pull-outs for children's toys and overflow from the kitchen," Elizabeth describes.

With the owners' fashion background and appreciation of colour, Elizabeth experimented with a bolder, more assertive palette in parts of the home. "The dining room walls are wrapped in an inky, almost black roman clay finish, while the study shines in 'Sulking Room Pink' by Farrow & Ball and the garden room glows in the warmth of a cedar-lined ceiling and deep-brown tiled walls," says Elizabeth. "However, I was careful to balance this with an array of neutrals in paint colour, textures and fabrics. They play a supporting role that unifies and softens the complexity and depth of colour throughout the house."

For Elizabeth, designing an artful and elegant home transcends aesthetics; it's about creating a sanctuary for the soul. "The cornerstones of beauty are fundamental to our quest to seek perfection—the standard that we judge our work and our dedication to our craft," Elizabeth says. This dedication to authenticity imbues Moore Park with a timeless sophistication, blending quiet grandeur, serenity and often the unexpected.

Napa Valley, California, United States

NAPA VALLEY HOUSE

Design studio K Interiors
Photography John Merkl

"Creatively, this was a dream project, especially because the owners wanted the interior decoration to be surprising, fun and to add a wow factor. Nothing could be pedestrian."
– Kristen Peña

Beyond its famous vineyards and vibrant cultural scene, California's Napa Valley enjoys a temperate climate and boasts a picturesque landscape with rolling hills covered in vines and surrounded by mountains. Located just an hour's drive north of San Francisco, it's no surprise that those seeking a quick escape from the city are drawn to the area. This is precisely why two executives from San Francisco purchased a 418-square-metre property there as a getaway home a few years ago.

To transform the outdated 1980s house, pool area and guesthouse into a stylish sanctuary, the couple enlisted Kristen Peña of K Interiors to design a comprehensive renovation plan. "I wanted to create a space that reflected the Napa experience for these homeowners while prioritising their lifestyle choices," says the designer. Accordingly, Kristen tailored the design to the couple's desire for a weekend respite from their hectic work life while providing them with a sumptuous and sophisticated social hub for friends to visit.

The four-bedroom property already boasted magnificent views and abundant natural light, but it was exceptionally bland from a designer's perspective. So, after completing building works, painting and renovating the kitchen and bathrooms, Kristen began the second phase of the project by decorating the rooms using an earthy colour palette and varied material textures. "The specific aim was to create an oasis of beauty, style and personality," says Kristen. "Creatively, this was a dream project, especially because the owners wanted the interior decoration to be surprising, fun and to add a wow factor. Nothing could be pedestrian."

Kristen created luxurious living environments by combining European elegance with contemporary American sensibilities, weaving a narrative that honoured the home's architectural lines while introducing playful elements. Then, reflecting on her clients' appreciation for contemporary art and high-end design pieces, she transformed the home into a gallery-like retreat, dotted with unique and functional sculptures, crafts and furniture. Bespoke pieces seamlessly merge form with function and celebrate imagination and individuality.

As Kristen's clients are well-travelled and passionate art collectors, the designer collaborated with them to infuse the space with newly sourced artworks, as well as unusual artefacts and design pieces bought specifically for the project. "I found some totems in an antique store in New York and positioned them in a corner of the main living area next to a Little Petra armchair by Viggo Boesen, and I hung work by California-based artist America Martin above a side table crafted by Casey McCafferty in the entry," says Kristen.

She selected each artisanal and designer piece to align with the concept of "provocative sensibility", from the large soft and organic fibre wall hanging by Mexican craft brand Caralarga in the entry to the sinuous wooden sculpture by Nicholas Shurey in the primary suite and the expressive Melt Mirror by Bower in the guest bedroom.

This idea also extended to more utilitarian rooms: Jung Lee's electric word-art photography is mounted on Gucci wallpaper in the laundry, and Joseph's stainless-steel artwork with a concrete-letter slogan hangs in the office bathroom.

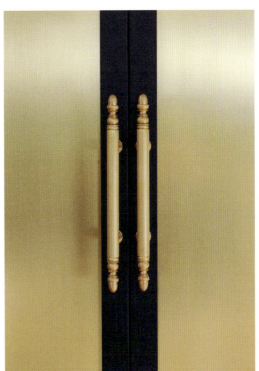

While artwork creates visual focal points in the home, Kristen's choice in interior furnishings underscored the interplay between craft and materiality, evident in shapely wood, brass and stone components. These feature throughout the house, with bespoke pieces such as a gold and black bar in the living room, and handcrafted ceramic shade lighting by Natalie Page suspended over a custom-made irregularly shaped table in the dining area. Martha Sturdy's undulating wall-mounted sculpture *Brass Landscape* adds another layer of craft and materiality to the dining room.

It was also essential that the interior design scheme have the sense of easy-living comfort that befits a holiday home. "One of our core values was delivering comfort as much as luxury," says Kristen. "This was achieved by introducing quality furnishings that integrate pattern and texture in their designs." The living room features a woven sisal-and-leather rug with a geometric pattern, complemented by curvy sofas upholstered in alpaca bouclé by Philippe Malouin, horsehair-fringed stools and a coffee table from Banda Gallery, with a travertine base and patinaed brass top.

In the softly grey-hued primary bedroom, a custom bed features an upholstered headboard, and Caroline Lizarraga's limewash wall treatment adds warmth to the room, as it does throughout the home. In the ensuite, the bathtub occupies prime position in the corner, where the view of the treetops out the window invites relaxation and quiet.

More tactile sensuality can be found in the guesthouse, where the primary bedroom features a woven bedhead and an earthy-toned macramé wall hanging by Sally England. Textural elements are also on display in the caramel-coloured office of the main house, with a puffed Amura sectional sofa in the sitting area and blush silk wallpaper on the ceiling. Above the sofa, Al Satterwhite's famous black-and-white photograph of Stevie Wonder takes centre stage and captures attention.

Working closely with the homeowners to ensure the interiors reflected her clients' love of art and entertaining, Kristen left no stone unturned to transform the home into a sanctuary of style. "It all came down to the details, balancing a mix of materials and textures while elevating the display of arts and craftworks."

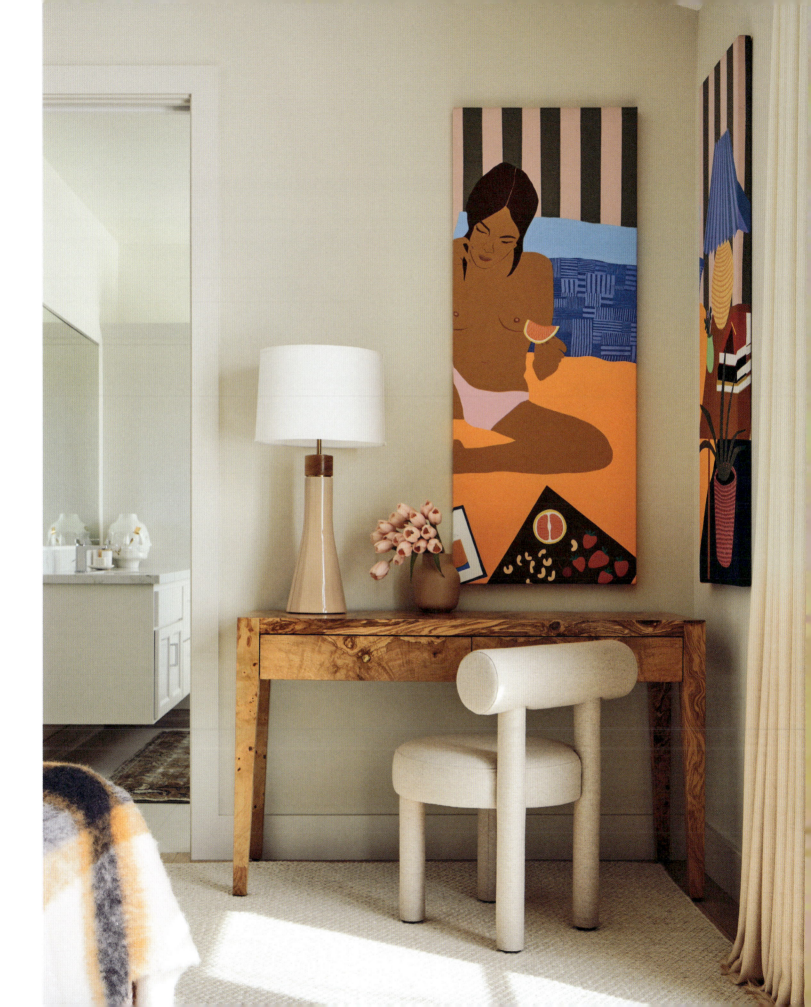

Museumkwartier, The Hague, The Netherlands

NEW SCHOOL RESIDENCE

Design studio Avenue Design Studio
Photography Avenue Design Studio

"What I particularly love about this home is the balance between the grandeur of the property and its rich history, and the sense of humbleness we instilled in each space."
– Holly Marder

New School Residence, in the centre of The Hague, is a former ballet school gracefully transformed into an elegant townhouse. This historical gem was slowly and meticulously brought back to life by Avenue Design Studio. Founder Holly Marder led her team to revive the property's period charm while infusing it with contemporary energy and a generous nod to the British roots of the expat homeowners.

"We consulted the homeowners on how to transform the internal spaces of the three-storey building into a stylish five-bedroom, three-bathroom family home for five," says Holly. Her team collaborated with Foam Architects, the firm tasked with the external and infrastructure renovations, and the construction team Euroconstruct, to ensure the renovation was meticulously crafted.

The ground floor welcomes visitors with Burgundy flagstones quarried from southern France, setting a tone of tradition and history while imparting warm tones and texture underfoot. The layout on this level includes an open-plan kitchen, dining and living area with views to a terraced garden.

Deftly bridging the gap between cosy design and pure style, the living room balances historic forms and poetic minimalism with comfort. The result is a bright, airy room with a mix of lines and curves that is especially inviting. "One of my absolute favourite spaces in the house is the cosy setting we created for the living room," says Holly.

An Obelisco travertine–clad fireplace, designed by the team at Avenue Design Studio, rises from the French limestone floors, creating a striking focal point. An olive-green velvet sofa, set upon a hemp rug, is paired with a wooden coffee table also designed by the studio. "We named the table Gyazā (meaning 'gather') in reference to the Japanese culture of gathering low to the ground for meals. It features traditional joinery and slats in whitened pine and introduces a *shizen* or 'natural' sensibility to the living space," Holly explains. Art from the studio's own A. Gallery, along with decorations from Fundamente, a Dutch-based gallery specialising in 20th-century furniture and objects, completes the scene.

Opposite, a semi-custom walnut kitchen in a traditional English Shaker style is enhanced with crystal marble benchtops and a discreet wrap-around breakfast bar. "The expressive veins of crystal marble add a little touch of drama to this humble kitchen, which I love," says Holly. "The luxe materials combined with the kitchen's simple style highlight how a blend of elegance and functionality can work to increase the benefits of living in a well-designed home."

Towards the rear of the ground floor is the dining room in which a commanding table, made from reclaimed pitch pine beams, and once part of the owners' former residence in the Peak District, is accompanied by Dordogne chairs designed by Charlotte Perriand.

This narrative of scale and tactility continues to the first floor, where the flooring scheme changes from functional flagstones to wood, evoking a feeling of understated luxury. "Rich oak herringbone parquetry graces the more classical upper floors where the bedrooms are located, setting a decidedly more opulent tone," Holly explains.

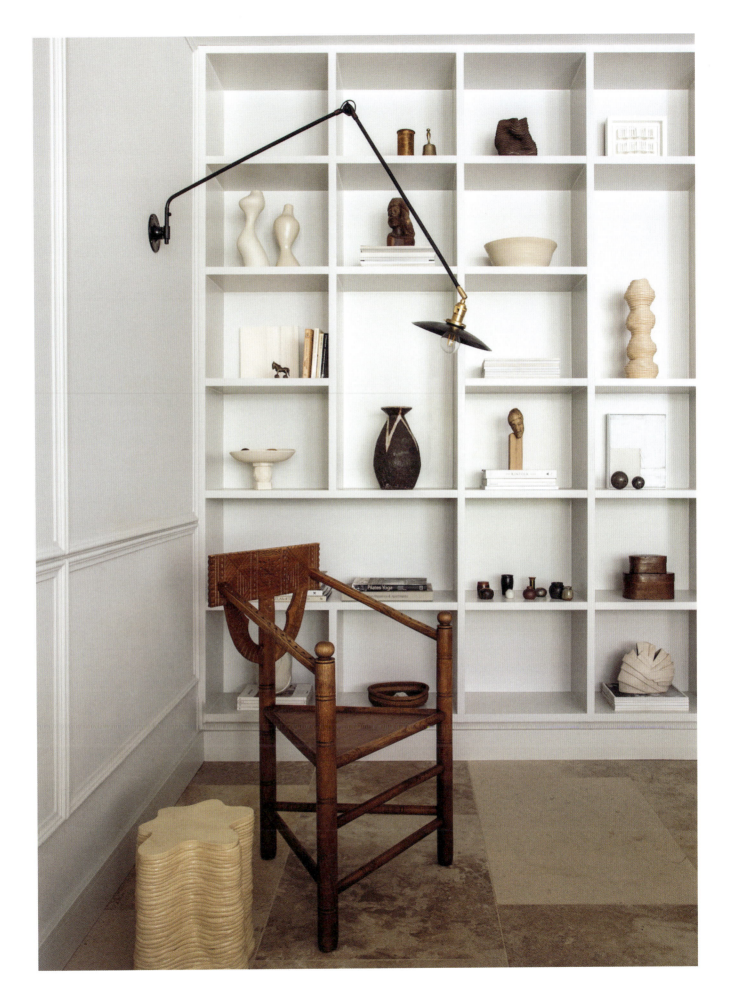

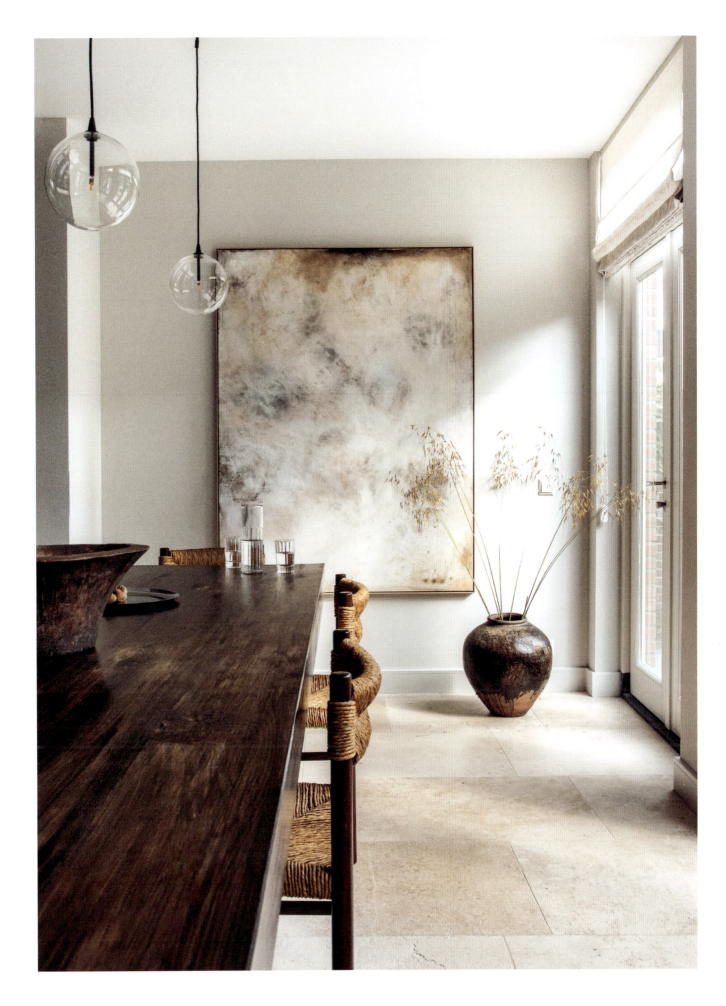

Partition doors were reintroduced between two adjoining spaces on the first floor, creating options for privacy or openness. They divide the primary bedroom suite from an informal living area, which is furnished with a pair of Colonial chairs designed by Ole Wanscher, a brass-wrapped coffee table, sculptural ceramics and contemporary abstract art.

In the primary bathroom, the custom walnut vanity is designed like a piece of furniture, with two basins resting on top, and the tapware, mirror and light fixtures positioned on the wall to emphasise symmetry. A vintage stool provides a neat and elegant side table next to a freestanding bath.

"Bespoke furniture design was also a large part of our scope for the project," Holly notes, emphasising the importance of personalised elements. "In the upstairs sitting room, we designed beautiful screens made of walnut and webbing to disguise radiators. We also crafted custom-fitted cabinetry on either side of the partition doors. On one side is a tidy but sleek bar cabinet featuring smoked mirror, Vienna white marble and brass detailing."

Like the floors, colour schemes subtly change from the lower to upper levels of the home. "We applied a cooler palette of soft grey and olive for the open-plan ground floor and paired these colours with warm-toned materials such as limestone, travertine and walnut to moderate the contemporary undercurrent," says Holly. "On the upper floors, we chose warmer tones for the walls to highlight traditional features and to create a cosy atmosphere in these more refined spaces."

Throughout New School Residence, a careful selection of furnishings and decorations also plays a crucial role in bringing Avenue Design Studio's vision to life. Vintage elements and unique pieces from Studio Nine Design, Studio Yen and Time & Style, alongside artworks by Geraldine Kol and Aliyah Sadaf, complete this exquisitely furnished house. "Together, these items add that final layer of harmony and contemporary elegance to bring the project to completion," says Holly.

"What I particularly love about this home is the balance between the grandeur of the property and its rich history, and the sense of humbleness we instilled in each space," says Holly. "There's nothing pretentious about this home, yet there's a sense of luxury to it in the choice of finishes and details throughout."

Los Angeles, California, United States

PACIFIC PALISADES RESIDENCE

Design studio DISC Interiors
Photography Sam Frost

"We believe well-designed homes have an energy that draws you in and comforts you for many years to come."
– David John Dick

Epitomising the finest aspects of Californian living, this newly built, three-storey family residence combines modern luxury with a welcoming ambience. Situated in the exclusive coastal neighbourhood of the Pacific Palisades in northwest Los Angeles, this spacious 1,152-square-metre property features six bedrooms and 10 bathrooms, as well as a guesthouse, a pool, a gym and a home theatre.

David John Dick and Krista Schrock, co-founders of DISC Interiors, known for their astute approach to high-end interior design, particularly in California, were tasked with transforming the residence into a sanctuary that perfectly blends the warmth of a family home with the sophistication of modern architecture. "The challenge of designing this house was a thrilling endeavour," says Krista. "Our clients, a creative family with a deep appreciation for art and design, wanted a space that was both functional for their everyday lives and perfect for entertaining. They wanted a family home that felt warm and textured, with beautiful lighting and a contemporary edge."

To produce the harmonious and inviting living environment, David and Krista collaborated with the owners and the build team so that every detail would be carefully considered. All furniture, lighting, wallpaper and window coverings were selected by DISC Interiors, while Fountainhead Homes, the architect and builder, handled the construction and design of the interior architecture.

Given the scope of work, there were some inevitable design conundrums for the DISC team to sort out. "One of the biggest challenges was to find the perfect lighting fixture for the entry," says David. "It's such a large, open space and it really sets the tone for the entire home. We commissioned Frederik Molenschot, an artist from Carpenters Workshop Gallery, to create a stunning handcrafted bronze and LED chandelier. The installation process was complex, but the result is a magnificent piece that can be admired from both the ground and first floors."

The entryway chandelier isn't the only stand-out feature. The dining room is adorned with green silk de Gournay wallpaper, which not only signals elegance and complements the green tones of the kitchen island, but seamlessly connects the interior spaces with the lush outdoor landscape. "We love the look and feel of silk wallpaper in this dining room with its dim lighting," says Krista, "It feels incredibly special to entertain in rooms like this. Spaces with balance and a feeling of calm appeal to us, so we aim to create rooms that invite guests to stay longer than they thought they would."

Located near the Pacific Ocean and surrounded by lush greenery, the home's serene setting deeply influenced its colour palette. Krista and David embraced the Mediterranean climate and the natural beauty of the area to create a nuanced journey of tonal discovery. "Earth tones and natural light, quintessential elements of California's landscape, played a significant role in our palette choices," says David. "We love the flow from room to room and how each space tells its own story while working as a whole."

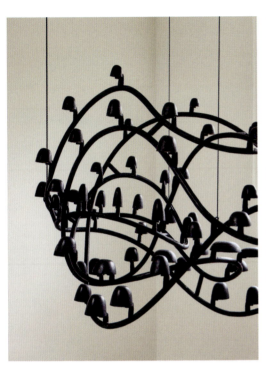

In selecting the materials and furniture, the designers prioritised comfort without compromising style. "Our philosophy in selecting furniture is that it must be comfortable for homeowners and their family and friends to sit in, relax, have conversations together, entertain, but still look smart," says Krista.

This reasoning is evident in various stone furniture pieces the designers commissioned Matt Castilleja to fabricate, including the entryway table, a breakfast table and a coffee table. "These pieces not only add a sculptural quality to the interiors but also balance the home's architectural volumes with their substantial presence," says David. Additionally, many pieces from DISC Interiors' own furniture collection are on show throughout the home, including the Jin Nightstand in the guest bedroom.

The extensive outdoor areas were also considered in the layout to foster a seamless transition between indoors and outdoors. "We wanted to emphasise the exterior patios and connect them to the interior living spaces," says David. "Large sliding glass doors allow for this connection, making the flow between the inside and outside effortless."

Next to the living room, the bar was designed for conversation, listening to music and enjoying an evening cocktail. "We wanted the room to feel timeless, mixing in elements of Art Deco and the 1920s, while still feeling contemporary. As this room opens to the living room, we wanted them to connect but also have a different function and palette," David explains. The walls are painted a rich eggplant colour to accent the Bongó bar cabinet by Greenapple and the antique brass tones.

This deep hue continues on the first floor, where it brings warmth and vibrancy to the client's study. "We love the play of the colour palette from the painted walls to the artwork by Filipa Tojal to the accent of the brass desk lamp," Krista says. The study, located off the primary bedroom, is a warm and textural space. The ensuite is equally layered and refined, with a vintage rug and resin side table crafted by Scala Luxury.

The idea of a home as a sanctuary guides much of the designers' ethos. "For us, calm and curated homes are a balance of materials, both hard and soft, and textures. We prefer a variety in materiality so the interiors do not feel static," says David. "We also love symmetry, and asymmetry. We apply this approach to furniture placement to loosen a room up."

Lighting also plays a crucial role in establishing a relaxed vibe. "A mixture of lamps, decorative lighting and ambient lighting ensures a soft, inviting glow rather than harsh, direct light," David says. "Handwoven throws, beautiful bedding, natural linens and velvets also contribute to the home's intimate, cosy ambience."

Ultimately, the success of the interior design for the Pacific Palisades home lies in how it works for the homeowners. "Knowing our clients love being in their home and how it makes them feel is the best reward," says Krista.

David agrees: "We believe well-designed homes have an energy that draws you in and comforts you for many years to come. They should be elegant, collected and artfully put together, but not seem overly decorated."

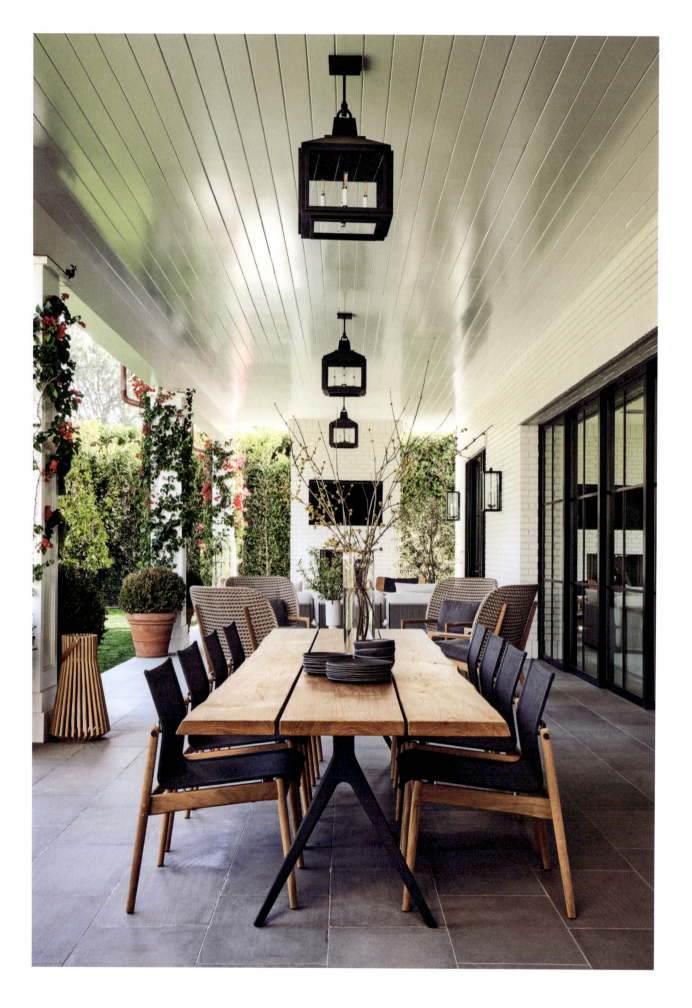

Île de la Cité, Paris, France

PLACE DAUPHINE PIED-À-TERRE

Design studio After Bach Studio
Photography Vincent Leroux

"I wanted the space to exude the feeling that all the decoration had been realised a long time ago."
– Francesco Balzano

Located in the coveted 1st arrondissement of Paris is a 17th-century-listed building on the Place Dauphine, a leafy triangular 'square' on the western tip of the Île de la Cité. On the third floor, a 180-square-metre pied-à-terre boasts views of the Seine and the iconic Pont Neuf, providing its owners, collectors of art and design, with a spacious apartment from which to enjoy the historic surroundings.

As the interiors were in need of an update, the owners appointed interior design studio After Bach to transform the home into a two-bedroom, two-bathroom sanctuary of refined living. For designer Francesco Balzano, whose ethos embodies an appreciation for art as a poetic lens to perceive the world, every detail would serve as a brushstroke on the canvas of this Parisian masterpiece of interior design. "Art is a way of seeing, a way of poetically inhabiting the world," he says, underscoring the studio's dedication to creating environments that transcend mere functionality.

From the outset, Francesco drew inspiration from luminaries of art and music, evoking the spirit of Cy Twombly's Roman abode, the evocative paintings of Balthus and the soulful melodies of Keith Jarrett. "We strive to create spaces like musical scores," says Francesco of his studio's practice. These influences imbue the apartment with character and cachet, setting the stage for a symphony of design elements to unfold.

Updating the historic space proved both exhilarating and daunting for Francesco as he queried how he would enhance the inherent beauty of such a location without overshadowing its rich heritage. The answer lay in crafting a design language of understated elegance, which spoke to the past while embracing the sophistication of the present.

"I wanted the space to exude the feeling that all the decoration had been realised a long time ago," Francesco explains. He gently peeled away layers of over-decoration and realigned the flow of the interior rooms. This produced a "feeling of harmony and space" and allowed for the focus to easily drift to the views of the river and bridge.

Francesco reconfigured the layout by uniting the living spaces. He accomplished this by linking each room via a light-filled hallway featuring large floor-to-ceiling shuttered windows overlooking the river on the Quai de l'Horloge roadway side. "The floor plan is designed in such a way as to organise the 'day' rooms—kitchen, dining room, living room, office and guest bedroom—on the Seine side. By reinforcing the vocabulary of a row of windows, and by positioning mirrors in the kitchen and arches elsewhere, this extended the spatial generosity and perspective," says Francesco.

The more intimate 'night' rooms are on the calmer Place Dauphine side, providing shelter from the hustle and bustle of the city. "The primary bedroom, for example, establishes a lyrical dialogue with the charm of Place Dauphine," says Francesco. "It's quite spacious and forms a private chamber with an ensuite bathroom that contains a pair of basins and a made-to-measure bathtub in solid stone."

One of Francesco's defining challenges was the restoration of the apartment's historic wooden herringbone floors, where a significant discrepancy in elevation posed a formidable obstacle. "There was a difference of 20 centimetres from a point at the top to a point at the bottom of the apartment," he says. It was important to lift and level the floorboards before any renovation took place. This work also provided an opportunity to integrate heating under the floor.

A palette of colours and materials, carefully selected to resonate with the essence of Paris, imbues each room with a sense of harmony and warmth. From the refined charm of bronze hardware and the sage-green lacquer that pays homage to the Seine, to the soft ivory tones of lime plaster, Parisian grey–coloured stone and ivory jute fabrics, every element speaks to the elegance of the city.

A recurring arch motif also permeates the apartment, adding an air of classicim and softening the rectilinearity of the rooms and hallway. Fransesco designed the fireplaces in the dining room and primary bedroom as bespoke versions of his own Mosaico collection, giving the fireplaces a more classical face with fluting to either side of the recessed arch.

In the living room, arches sculpted out of the wall behind the joinery are intended to imbue the space with a Villa Medici touch. In the library, a series of arched alcoves have stone drawers integrated at their base. "The idea was to give the sensation that it was all original but also new," Francesco explains. "The walls are covered with a Holland & Sherry bronze colour and linen fabric to give an authentic atmosphere."

But perhaps it is in the selection of furniture that the true essence of After Bach's design approach best shows how modernity and history intertwine. Francesco collaborated with Galerie JAG to craft a careful fusion of old and new, and included pieces by Francesco, Studio Floris Wubben, Frédéric Imbert and Rick Owens, alongside vintage treasures such as the Paolo Buffa armchair and Jacques Quinet daybed. The result is an atmosphere of comfort and pleasure.

The apartment now exudes an aura of quiet luxury, offering a welcoming entrance, before opening to a series of meticulously curated living spaces and sleeping quarters, all with views of the Seine. As Francesco reflects, "The precision of details, the mixture of noble materials, pure lines and the sublimation of the essential functions of everyday life are my signature."

Queen's Park, London, United Kingdom

QUEEN'S PARK TERRACE

Design studio Studio Skey
Photography Taran Wilkhu

"We've created a quiet and restful retreat through an organic process of transformative ideas, resulting in a comfortable, harmonious space that allows the family to feel nurtured and restful."
– Sophie Scott

Classic Victorian-era terraces line the leafy streets of Queen's Park in northwest London, their façades often characterised by ornamental red brickwork and bay windows. The interiors are equally distinctive, offering inhabitants enviable proportions and voluminous rooms with tall ceilings. One such house, purchased as a family home, had unfortunately lost much of its Victorian character due to an insensitive modernisation. To restore the grandeur of the original terrace, the new owners enlisted the expertise of interior design practice Studio Skey to oversee a comprehensive internal renovation.

With a brief that the home should exhibit an elegant balance between classic architecture and modern refinement, the designers Sophie Scott and Georgina Key meticulously reinstated the home's original detailing and wall mouldings, including cornices, architraves and skirtings. "Our aim was to restore the home's Victorian grandeur and fuse it with sleek, contemporary elements," says Sophie.

To suit the needs of the owners, a young family of four, Studio Skey's renovation of the four-storey, 232-square-metre property required a reconfigured layout plus a contemporary rear kitchen addition with an expansive glass roof. "The design concept for the property was to introduce plenty of light, a connection of relaxation spaces, and include five bedrooms and five bathrooms," Sophie explains.

One of the biggest challenges the designers faced was opening up the ground floor to create an open-plan kitchen, dining and living space. "We had to ensure that the large scale of the space, with ceilings more than 3 metres high, would not impact on the living area feeling warm and unified," says Georgina. The design solution included a step down into the new extension housing the kitchen and informal breakfast area. "Light from the large expanses of glazing now fills the space but also permeates the adjoining formal dining room, which features wall panelling, large artworks and a bespoke oak table for entertaining," says Georgina. "We also included a partial opening from the dining room into the living room to retain the Victorian character and allow for the potential future addition of doors."

Walking through the ground floor, the open-plan living, dining and kitchen area now extends into a courtyard garden. The first floor houses three bedrooms and a family bathroom, while the second floor includes the primary bedroom with ensuite, as well as a guest bathroom, an office and a dressing area. The top floor is a self-contained loft suite comprising a guest bedroom and bathroom.

The studio meticulously designed the wall panelling throughout the house to work with a variety of artwork sizes. "We always knew we wanted a triptych to sit within the three panels in the dining room and the piece by Alexandria Coe worked beautifully in the space," says Georgina. "The scale and height was perfect and we loved the natural forms and loose representation of Alexandria's soft charcoal work on raw cotton canvas." They were framed in a dark walnut that complements the custom dining table.

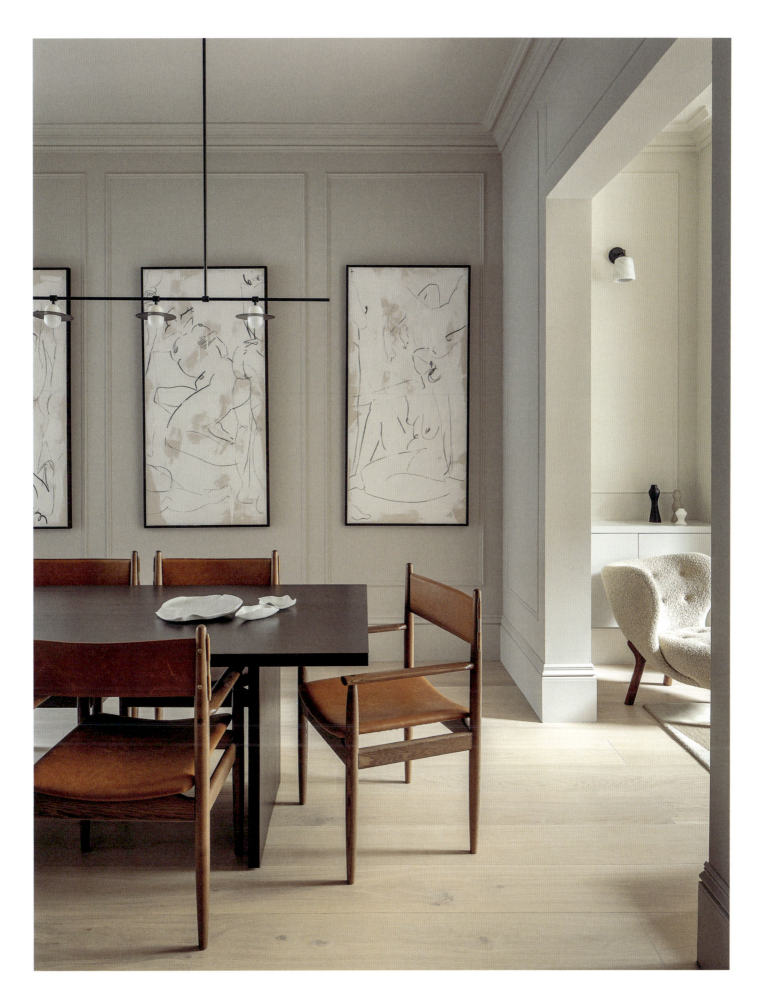

The home's artwork selection includes pieces by Alexandra Yan Wong and Greg Wood, along with other artists. "We chose the artworks that work tonally with the soft earthy palette and that depict abstract scenes by artists who use organic mediums, textures and markings that blend seamlessly with the rest of the scheme formed with natural, textured materials," Georgina says.

The design aesthetic for the home was inspired by Studio Skey's previous work on the clients' offices located in a Georgian townhouse in Marylebone. "We carried the same refined palette of muted greys into their Queen's Park home, complementing the soft colours with natural furnishings, like richly textured rugs and earth-toned fabrics, to create a warmer, more inviting space," says Georgina. "We also added sympathetic contrasts via high-end materials, such as dark-stained oak, honed marbles, unlacquered brass and brushed oak floors."

The studio designed bespoke joinery pieces, particularly for the kitchen, which features unique cross-sawn oak-front cupboards. In the primary suite, they installed a wall with framed linen panels to conceal a television and added floor-to-ceiling wardrobes in a generous walk-in dressing room.

"We introduced some beautiful natural stone into this project," says Sophie. "Honed Taj Mahal quartzite is used for the kitchen countertops, while Silk Georgette marble adorns the primary bathroom. The marble's softly blurred striations feature extensively in the shower stall, architrave detail, skirting and vanity top. Complemented by a cocoon-like freestanding bath, brass tapware, high ceilings with Victorian plaster coving and a large sash window, the room exudes understated luxury."

Elsewhere, a curated selection of high-quality furniture and fixtures emphasises comfort and durability, while simultaneously creating a sophisticated yet welcoming environment. The living room features the Tor Tailored Sofa from Sedilia, the Ryo chair by Hans Hansen & Son and Viggo Boesen's Little Petra armchair, all chosen for their soft curves and tactile upholstery in warm mustard, cream and rust hues. At the centre, a round Cosmos travertine coffee table from Atelier278 sits on a soft pink rug by Anni Albers, while a custom mitred Fume Emperador marble fireplace adds formality. Long, relaxed linen curtains frame the expansive bay window, paired with sheer linen curtains to diffuse sunlight and add privacy.

In high-traffic areas, the designers specified darker, earth-toned, hard-wearing furnishing fabrics. "The banquette in the kitchen is upholstered in an espresso-brown child-friendly outdoor fabric to repel any stains at dinner time," says Georgina. "The oversized cushions add softness and create comfortable seating for the family."

By curating a layout tailored to their clients' lifestyle and incorporating a calming tonal palette with rich textures and natural materials, Studio Skey created a family sanctuary in busy London. Sophie and Georgina both agree that central to their design was a gentle, poetic approach. "We've created a quiet and restful retreat through an organic process of transformative ideas, resulting in a comfortable, harmonious space that allows the family to feel nurtured and restful," says Sophie.

Irvine, California, United States

SHADY CANYON RESIDENCE

Design studio Huma Sulaiman Design
Photography Shade Degges

"We took inspiration from the natural surroundings—the cactus and green shrubbery—and chose complementary tones that would blend seamlessly with the environment."
– Huma Sulaiman

Seeking to modernise their newly purchased property in Irvine's lush Shady Canyon community, a couple with a young family engaged Huma Sulaiman Design to masterfully transform their 1,208-square-metre Mediterranean-style home into a luxurious yet comfortable family haven.

The scope of the renovation included the redesign of expansive living and dining areas, two kitchens, a primary bedroom with his-and-hers bathrooms and walk-in wardrobes, three children's bedrooms, a playroom, multiple bathrooms and a basement with a bar, theatre and sauna. Designer Huma Sulaiman utilised neutral tones, natural materials and undulating forms to create a contemporary three-storey family home that radiates elegance while ensuring functionality.

"When our clients bought this home, the interior was dated. They wanted a total overhaul," says Huma. The brief was clear: design a stylish, sophisticated interior that would not only reflect the clients' discerning tastes, but also provide a safe and inviting environment for their children. Soft, rounded-edge furniture, unique light fixtures and a muted colour palette were top priorities.

Having worked with the family previously, Huma understood their preferences and vision, allowing her to create a space that would celebrate distinctive materiality and sculptural form. "I've come to know this couple quite well over the years," Huma explains. "I worked on a previous home of theirs when they were just a family of two. Now they have three young children. However, it was essential to create a home that was both sophisticated and child-friendly."

Huma's selection of high-quality, durable finishes and materials for floors, benchtops and walls was crucial for achieving the desired balance of comfort, sophistication and practicality. "We preferred performance fabrics for upholstery as they could withstand the inevitable spills and mishaps of family life," she says.

The clients asked Huma to source furniture pieces that had soft edges and were safe for their young children to play around. "We naturally gravitated towards pieces that are rounded and low in height, as well as plush in material, which all brings comfort and welcomes one to the space." Soft, curved edges on low-slung modular seating, such as the olive-green velvet Tufty-Time sectional sofa by Patricia Urquiola in the informal sitting room, and the plush Camaleonda sectional sofa by Mario Bellini in the formal living room, ensure safety for the children while maintaining a stylish aesthetic.

"Our clients wanted their daughter's bed to be directly on the ground, but we couldn't find anything suitable, so we designed our own," Huma shares. "Our bespoke scalloped bed with upholstered headboard, placed on a platform, was an instant hit. The pretty florals in the Gucci wallpaper and on our custom rug design adds a whimsical element, too."

Bespoke design is a hallmark of Huma's stylistic approach. In addition to some furniture pieces, her team designed every cabinet in the house, from the kitchens and bathrooms to the walk-in wardrobes and cupboards and large bar in the basement. "We pride ourselves on custom design; no details are overlooked," says Huma. "In 'her' primary bathroom, all the drawers in the vanity were designed to fit my client's extensive collection of makeup. We also designed a custom light fixture in the form of a chandelier for the bar area."

One of the most significant challenges in the renovation was a series of classical pillars dominating the main living areas and the foyer. These structural elements clashed with the clients' modern aesthetic. Huma's solution was innovative and transformative, making them a star feature. "We clad the pillars with wood planks, gave them a rectangular shape and finished them in trowelled plaster with a raked, or fluted, appearance," Huma explains. "This added a subtle yet striking detail to the entry of the home and enhanced the divide between the entry, living and dining zones without overwhelming the space. What was once an eyesore has become the most admired architectural detail in the renovation."

Plaster played a pivotal role in the visual success of the design plan elsewhere. It was used extensively on walls, ceilings, fireplace surrounds and interior arches, referencing a repetition of softly undulating shapes throughout the home. In the living room alone, organic and curvaceous forms can be seen in the sculptural artwork *Waltz* by Chris Baas above the fireplace, the travertine coffee table from Hommés Studio, and the stacked Neru wood stools by Rebeca Cors that stand as a totem in the corner.

"The home is distinguished by sleek European furnishings and iconic pieces of furniture and lighting teamed with antiques, art and local artisans' craft, along with some of our custom designs," says Huma, whose team sources decor from all over the world. The result is a home where every piece of furniture invites comfort and relaxation, and each object and artwork fosters contemplation and reflection.

For the home's colour scheme, Huma drew inspiration from a nearby nature reserve, opting for colours that complement the lush greenery and rugged canyon views. Shades of olive, rust, green, pale pink and off-white dominate the home, creating a serene, cohesive atmosphere. "My clients love colour but wanted it employed in a very subtle way. We took inspiration from the natural surroundings—the cactus and green shrubbery—and chose complementary tones that would blend seamlessly with the environment," Huma explains.

The transformation of the Shady Canyon property into a stylish and inviting residence where every detail has been thoughtfully curated to create a calming sanctuary for living is a fitting example of comfort-focused design. "To see how we have morphed this large project into a young family's dream home, where every weekend there are kiddy gatherings or sophisticated adult evening soirees, is heartwarming. To know that the family is creating beautiful memories in their home is our ultimate satisfaction," says Huma.

Brooklyn, New York, United States

STATE STREET TOWNHOUSE

Design studio Frederick Tang Architecture
Photography Gieves Anderson

"The heart of this project was to create a warm environment that welcomes the family and their friends, but is still stylish and modern."
– Barbara Reyes

Charming brownstones and row houses characterise the family-friendly neighbourhood of historic Boerum Hill in Brooklyn, New York. On one of the area's prettiest tree-lined streets, a young family of four found their dream home within a 325-square-metre Georgian-style row house. With the house in dire need of an update, the family appointed Frederick Tang Architecture (FTA) to transform it into a cohesive, modern space. The result: a stylish and sophisticated property reorganised to accommodate the needs of a busy family while balancing intimate areas with communal zones.

Upon entering the home, the eye is immediately drawn to an impressive fireplace in the double-height living area. "Creating a curving sculptural form for the fireplace was one of my favourite moments in this project," says Frederick Tang, FTA's founder and principal. "We were inspired by the plasterwork of artist Valentine Schlegel, but wanted to find something that would simultaneously draw your eye up to appreciate the lofty entry space while still creating an intimate seating area." The fireplace, a dramatic centrepiece, is integrated into a custom entry bench with tambour siding and upholstery by both Maharam and Pollack. This streamlined feature anchors the 6-metre-high ceilings and wall of south-facing windows.

Another sculptural element in the home is a central, curved plaster staircase that connects all the levels of the three-bedroom and three-and-a-half-bathroom townhouse. "The staircase spirals up, offering moments of pause at each level, where there is whimsical wallpaper or an unexpected change in material from plaster to custom reeded-glass and brass stair rails," says FTA's director of interior design, Barbara Reyes. "Both the staircase and fireplace create a wonderful sense of movement throughout the house, which unifies the whole."

Adjacent to the dramatic living area is a sophisticated dining room, where Frederick had the existing faux traditional ceiling and trim detailing removed, updating it to something more modern. A rounded inset ceiling now defines the dining space, spotlighting a geometric brass and marble chandelier from Cosulich Interiors & Antiques. On the wall of the dining area is a large painting from the client's grandmother, complementing an antique black-marble and brass dining table from vintage store Eunique Space, a burgundy bench from the Danish Design Store and blush-pink dining chairs by Mambo Unlimited Ideas.

The ground floor flows seamlessly from the open-plan living room to a walk-though kitchen that leads out to a lush garden and outdoor entertaining area. The kitchen now features a custom-fabricated black marble island by Casa Quieta, a Hurricane Black marble backsplash and a state-of-the-art AGA range. "The palette here is predominantly black and cream with integrated jewel tones of peacock blue, rust, oxblood, mulberry, wine and blush. The richness is offset by lots of brass—a request of the client," says Barbara.

A selection of exquisite stone is a key element in both the kitchen and elsewhere. Breccia Pernice marble forms a custom vanity in the powder room and a benchtop for the top-floor bar, both complemented by painterly wallpaper. In the living room, elegant brown quartzite complements the entry millwork and the plaster fireplace.

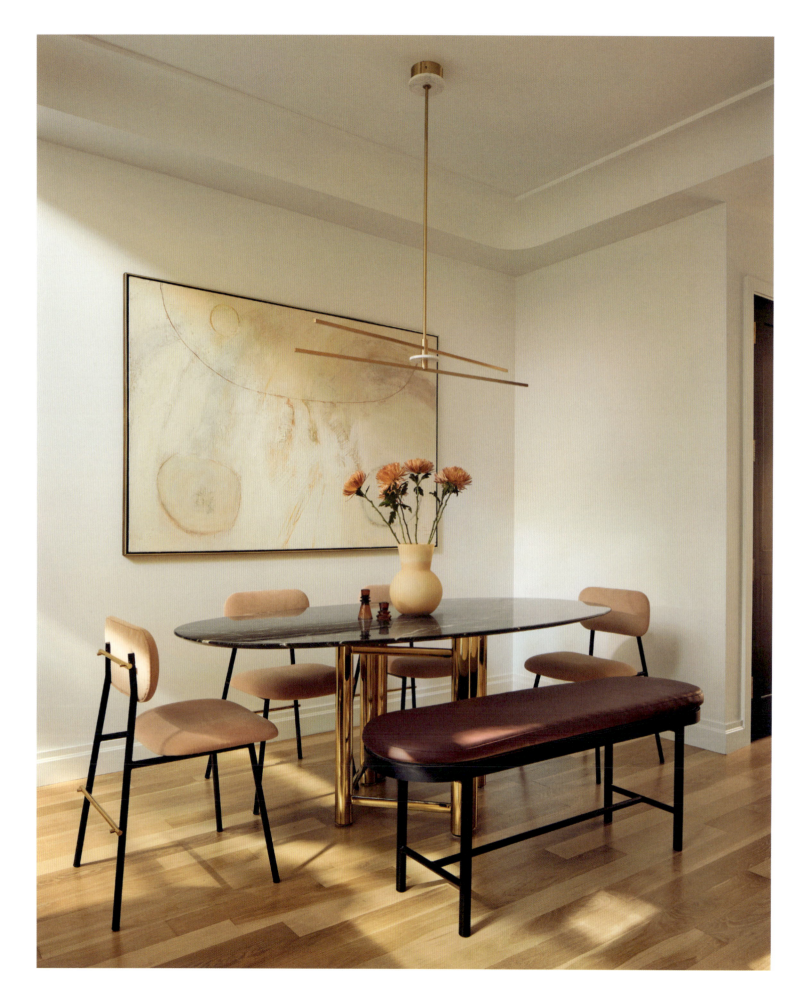

The sinuous plaster staircase ascends to the first floor, which opens into another double-height living room accented by a wall of windows. "The first time we walked through the house, we could all see the challenges of updating the home, but were also excited by the potential of these dramatic double-height spaces," says Frederick. This second living space features an L-shaped sofa once belonging to the client's late grandmother. It's positioned alongside a vintage swivel cocktail table in black glass and brass, and a Slash Objects end table made of concrete, rubber and brass. Lighting includes wall sconces by Atelier de Troupe and a pendant from Circa Lighting.

Also on this floor is a cosy bar area that was ingeniously created in a previously under-utilised dark hallway. FTA transformed it into a social nook and wet bar with a purposefully darker palette than the adjacent living room. "Strategic design assisted in partitioning these two areas visually and functionally, while the palettes we chose gave distinction and personality to each space," says Barbara. To further define the bar area, custom-painted de Gournay wallpaper in bold black, beige and gold, and shimmering with metallic thread, complements tambour-fronted fluted millwork cladding the bar, and luxurious russet-coloured velvet upholstery on a long, tufted bench seat.

The second floor houses the primary bedroom, which is the couple's favourite room. The serene space is lined with a custom cream-coloured wallpaper by Sarkos, and features blue watercolour–patterned drapery from Eskayel curtaining three large bay windows. A curved, blush-coloured side chair in the corner invites one to sit and read, adding to the room's tranquil ambience. "We designed this as a parent sanctuary," says Barbara.

The ascent to the top floor is a testament to the playful use of wallpaper throughout the house. A handpainted, floral-patterned wallpaper by Artemest lines the stairwell, and is notable for its black, blush and green tones. It was chosen for its tie-in with the plant-filled outdoor terrace on this level. This floor also houses a dedicated work-from-home area, a necessity for the modern family.

The FTA team has created a home that is smart and welcoming. "Our design philosophy for residential properties, whether new build, upgrade or complete renovation, relies on careful proportions and changes in scale," explains Frederick. "We want to create areas within the house that feel open, generous and filled with light, balanced by more intimate, cosy areas where residents can feel cocooned."

This is especially evident in State Street Townhouse, where the family now enjoy spaces custom designed for intimate family moments or grand gatherings. "The heart of this project was to create a warm environment that welcomes the family and their friends, but is still stylish and modern. Harmonious in colour, texture and form, the design we created is loved by the family and makes them feel happy," says Barbara.

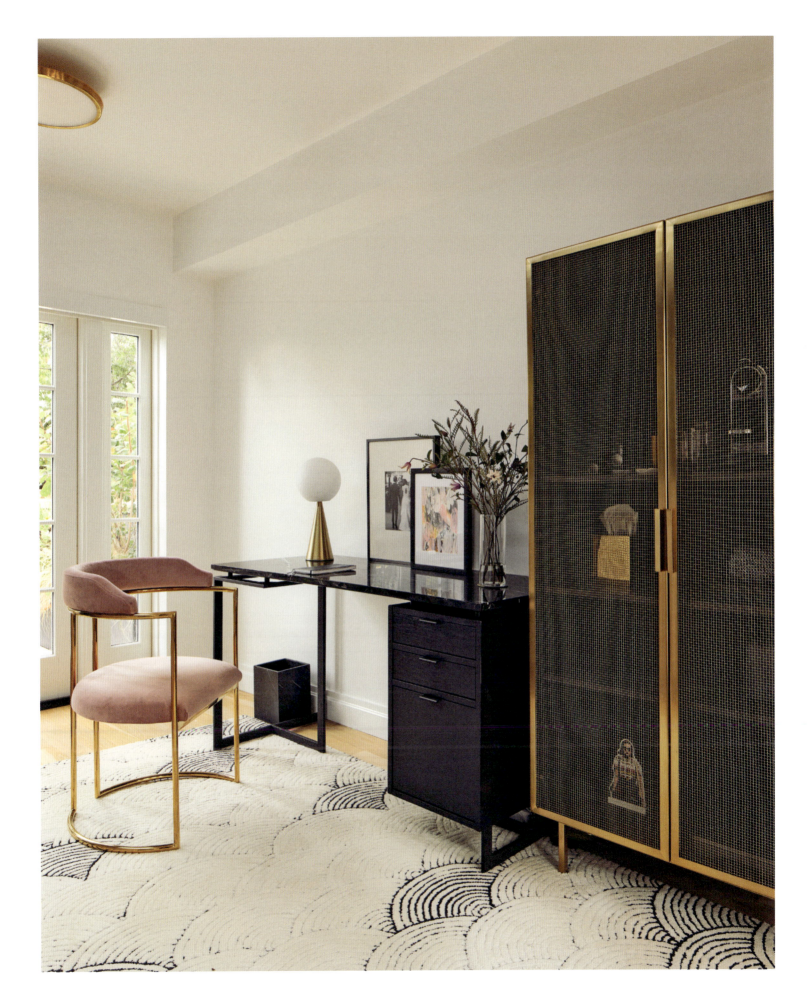

Östermalm, Stockholm, Sweden

STOCKHOLM RESIDENCE

Design studio AO/JN Interiors
Photography Kristofer Johnsson

"We wanted to find a balance between old and new and maintain the subtle classical feel typical to the 1920s, without leaning too much on overly extravagant classical details."
– Jesper Nyborg

When a family of four sought to renovate their Stockholm apartment located in a heritage-listed 1920s building, they turned to Alexandra Ogonowski and Jesper Nyborg of design studio AO/JN Interiors to craft a sensitive remodel. Favouring an elegant but slightly minimalist aesthetic, the design pair transformed the space into a seamless integration of the past and present, and of form and beauty, creating a harmonious sanctuary in the heart of the city.

"The nature of Swedish 1920s architecture means it isn't as decorated or ornate as turn-of-the-century style architecture," says Jesper. "But we still wanted to find a balance between old and new and maintain the subtle classical feel typical to the 1920s without leaning too much on overly extravagant classical details. Instead, we introduced these features in a subtle, elegant way that blended nicely with the new, modern design features of the apartment."

From the outset, Alexandra and Jesper aimed to retain the heritage essence while infusing modernity throughout the apartment. The custom joinery, with thin MDF panelling, served as a nod to the building's heritage while maintaining a contemporary ambience. This delicate balance was particularly evident in the transformed floor plan.

"In terms of the spatial layout, we were challenged by a long and narrow living room," says Jesper. "We decided to divide it up, turning one part into a welcoming entry or foyer while the rest of the space formed the new living room. We also changed the location of the existing kitchen, previously renovated in the 1960s, to create a larger, more open space connected to the dining room."

As one enters the apartment, the first impression is the circular foyer adorned with wall panelling that subtly conceals a frameless door leading to a powder room. "As a contrast to the apartment's overall warm neutral tonal palette, we installed black-and-white Breccia marble on the floor, creating a striking graphic element as soon as you enter the home," says Alexandra. "The use of contrasting materials or something unexpected is a common feature in our projects."

A custom-designed bench seat in walnut follows the curvature of the entry and offers storage, while a custom walnut and travertine circular table stands in the centre of the adjacent space, acting as a focal point and enhancing the welcoming ambience. "A beautiful Apparatus Cloud light hangs above the table, serving as a floating sculpture, and two Colonial chairs provide occasional seating," says Jesper.

The designers clad openings or transitions between living spaces with travertine marble slabs with step-back detailing on the edges. "The design of these 'portals' is made up of travertine slabs that step back to create depth," says Alexandra. "It gives a subtle nod to the more classical features in the home."

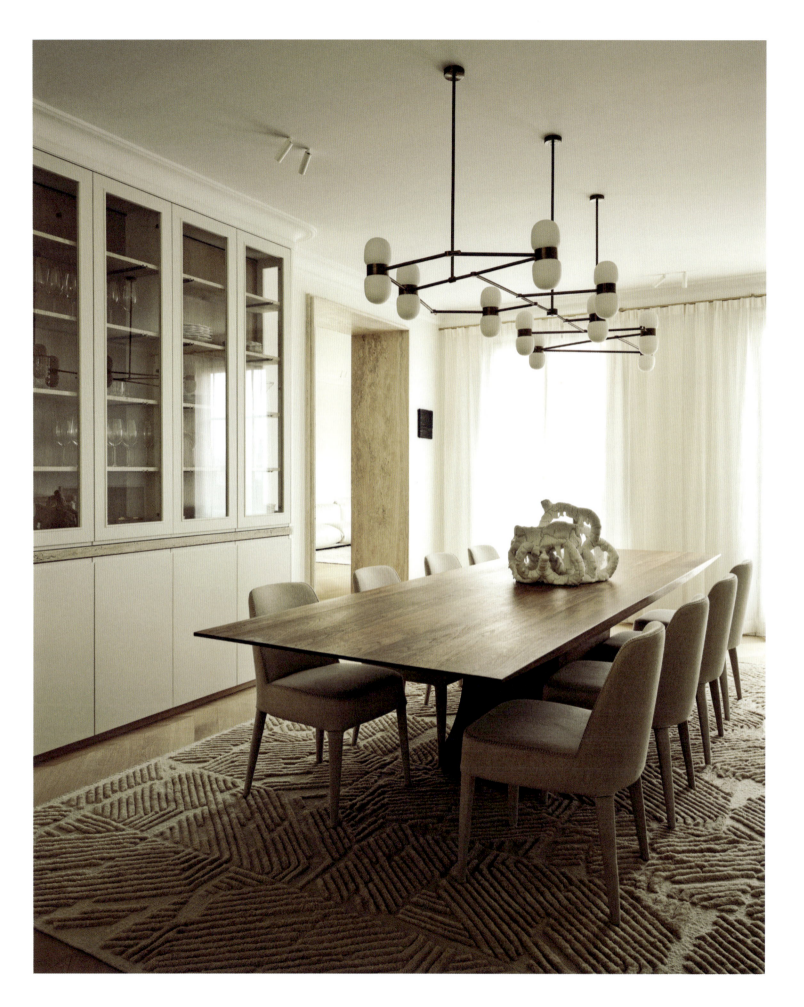

The eclectic mix of furniture and decor highlights the thoughtful curation throughout the apartment. In the living room, the Marenco sofa by Arflex, travertine coffee tables and Knutmattor rug complement the Apparatus pendant lights and wall sconces. The uncoventional steel mesh chair by Shiro Kuramata appears delicate and transparent, while the sculpture *Giant Gadroon* by Maxwell Mustardo from gallery Odem Atelier adds visual interest to the corner of the room.

In the dining room, another of AO/JN's furniture pieces has been custom designed for the apartment. "The shape of the walnut dining table is inspired by old blacksmith equipment, with the tabletop tapering back from its centre, creating a floating appearance," says Alexandra. Above, a custom Nuvol Chandelier by Mallorca lighting company Contain illuminates the space, framed by bespoke joinery for storing porcelain and wine glasses.

The clients expressed a particular desire for serenity, light and harmony in the kitchen. The new design is distinguished by curved ends and edges on the benchtops and cabinetry, adding softness, a theme that continues with the rangehood and ceiling cornices around the joinery. "We wanted the kitchen to echo established architectural treatments and colourways featured in other rooms, so we installed handpainted cupboard fronts with subtle MDF panelling," says Alexandra. "This, combined with the exquisite Calacatta marble, creates a harmonious atmosphere."

The primary bathroom reflects the home's refined aesthetic and also combines Calacatta stone and MDF panelling with curved edges, complemented by Articolo sconces and a travertine-clad bathtub as the centrepiece. "We continued the Calacatta marble on the floor and on the wall behind the double shower," says Jesper. "The step-back detailing almost gives the illusion of an artwork, thanks to the book-matched slabs and their pattern." Rendered plaster walls, using the traditional Moroccan technique of *tadelakt*, add a textural softness to the otherwise hard surfaces.

In the primary bedroom, plush textures abound with wall-to-wall carpet, fine bed linens and a custom headboard. The designers created bespoke open and closed storage, integrating the joinery with the architecture through panelling on the wall and cupboard fronts. "We also designed an 'island' in light oak as a seat and storage; a banquette seat in Calacatta Monet marble topped with softly toned fabric cushioning; and yet another fixture that functions as a desk or dressing table, with drawers underneath and a mirror above," says Alexandra.

The family home AO/JN Interiors has created in this urban apartment exhibits high-quality design and sophistication yet still feels soft, comforting and warm, thanks to the combination of textures, rounded shapes and bespoke details.

Yorkville, Toronto, Canada

SUBDUED SOPHISTICATION CONDOMINIUM

Design studio Nunu Interior Design
Photography Lauren Miller

"Our goal was to reflect quality through finishes and workmanship without over-layering. This meant choosing materials and furnishings that exuded a sense of timelessness and durability."
– Chantal Philippe

Known for its upscale restaurants, fashion boutiques and vibrant cultural scene, Yorkville in Toronto is a fashionable address, providing the perfect environment for those seeking an urban lifestyle. This dynamic inner-city neighbourhood also features an eclectic mix of architecture, including office buildings, upmarket hotels, attractive Victorian homes and, increasingly, luxury condominium apartments.

On the 12th floor of one such residential block is a sophisticated single-level condo designed by Chantal Philippe of Nunu Interior Design and Elyssa Myers. The 123-square-metre apartment with city views features two bedrooms with ensuites, plus a powder room. It is home to a young professional with a passion for travel and a keen eye for design—traits the designers felt made him an ideal client for this project.

The brief was clear from the start. "The space needed a full gut job; not a single thing was to remain," Chantal recalls. "Despite the limitations of working within a condo, where moving or opening up walls wasn't an option, we began by stripping everything down to the studs and redesigning from there."

The design aesthetic aimed to achieve a sophisticated, masculine look balanced by elements of warmth and comfort. "We wanted to avoid a sterile environment. Our goal was to reflect quality through finishes and workmanship without over-layering. This meant choosing materials and furnishings that exuded a sense of timelessness and durability," says Chantal.

One of the biggest challenges during the renovation was working with existing structural elements that had to remain. "However, being present onsite, working with a great team, creating mock-ups and exploring all options before sign-off, helped us overcome these obstacles," says Chantal. Despite the architectural constraints of the apartment, innovation flourished in the design process. Working around the existing bones of the building meant getting creative with the layout, its flow and general use of space.

Materiality played a crucial role in achieving the desired level of sophistication. To this end, the team used natural stone, wood veneers and custom herringbone floors. "One particularly pleasing application is the wood finish around openings. This creates a beautiful frame around the sightlines and perspectives within the space. Though tricky to apply, the wall trims are a good example of how details add stylistic value," says Chantal.

Arriving at the chosen colour palette was also a collaborative process. "Our client wanted a masculine look but was initially concerned that the space wasn't large enough for a moodier palette, especially one that scaled from beige through smoky brown to black, Once he saw our mock-ups and reference images showing what we envisaged, he trusted the process and allowed us to proceed with our ideas," explains Chantal.

The final colour scheme created the cocooning atmosphere the designers had envisioned and was particularly evident in the kitchen. "I love that the client allowed us to go dark with the kitchen finishes," says Chantal of the all-black stone countertops and the backsplash, a textured porcelain slab in a slate finish from Neolith. "Both provide framing for the dark oak cabinetry," she says.

In the bathroom, Chantal's moody material choices continue with Calacatta Viola marble selected for the vanity, a striking stone that displays elegant swirls of deep burgundy veining. "Many fear dark or bold colours, but in this condo they provide a unique yet cosy environment," Chantal describes.

Furniture selection was another area where the client's understanding of design and quality came into play. "He had specific brands in mind, which made sourcing easier," says Chantal. She focused on longevity and comfort, making numerous visits to the furniture stores to curate the perfect pieces.

Two favourites are the iconic Shell Chair, designed by Hans Wegner and produced by Carl Hansen & Søn, and the Gubi Beetle dining chairs around the table. Adding further refinement to the dining setting, a Cloud 19 pendant light designed by Apparatus hangs overhead, emitting a soft glow from its frosted glass orbs. The classic and enduring Eames Lounge Chair and Ottoman were owned by the client's mother and now take pride of place in a corner of the condo.

The design team also closely consulted their client when it came to the decor. "He loves art, so at the beginning of the project we considered all the places we could display his collection," says Chantal. "Even in the kitchen there are old portraits and still-life compositions displayed on the shelves."

One of her favourites is the large *Suite Tabou* lithograph by Jean-Paul Riopelle, which is hung conspicuously in the main living room where it is seen immediately upon entry. "The abstract composition features chaotic and intensely worked lines and patterns on paper mounted in a black frame and seems to align with the wall panelling on which it hangs," says Chantal.

The collaboration between the Nunu Interior Design team and their client has resulted in a home that not only meets but exceeds expectations. "As a minimalist, our client also wanted everything functional to be hidden in clever cabinetry," says Chantal. "We've successfully done this, creating a calming sanctuary tailored specifically to his needs."

Chantal, who now leads a talented team of five young women eager to make their mark on the design world, titled this project Subdued Sophistication, a worthy name for this compact condo and its stylishly elegant design.

Glebe, Sydney, Australia

TOXTETH TERRACE

Design studio: Jillian Dinkel
Photography Pablo Veiga

"I love how much the home reflects our beautiful clients' personalities. Every room speaks to their taste in a classic and timeless aesthetic."
– Jillian Dinkel

Displaying a harmonious blend of historical charm and modern elegance, Toxteth Terrace is a Victorian-era residence nestled in Sydney's inner-city neighbourhood of Glebe. The house was built in 1886 and spans 275 square metres. "The terrace is part of the heritage Toxteth Park estate, one of the first European developments in Glebe," says Jillian Dinkel, the designer responsible for the home's interior renovation, in collaboration with architect Troy Newman.

Jillian's interior design practice specialises in reimagining period homes in a contemporary context. For this home, Jillian's brief was to craft a comfortable oasis within a bustling inner-city environment for a busy family of five. "While calming tones, luxurious fabrics and a nod to luxury hotel living was crucial, having separate spaces for everyone in the family to retreat to and unwind was equally important," says the designer.

The design aesthetic conceived for the project aimed to be timeless, honest and natural, with finishes and decoration that would encourage relaxation. "A layering of the history of the home and the personal interests of our clients was key," Jillian says. "I wanted to create spaces that begged one to linger a bit longer, featuring elements that added a sense of wonder."

Respecting and maintaining the terrace's heritage attributes was a priority for both Jillian and her clients, particularly in the formal front rooms. Ceiling roses, fireplaces, sash windows, skirtings and cornices remain intact, while black iron-lace balustrades on the balcony and front entry were repaired. These features were also considered when it came to the contemporary rear addition. "We wanted to celebrate those elements throughout the home. We did this by referencing these details and sensibilities in the modern extension," Jillian explains.

This was thoughtfully achieved by incorporating arches between rooms; choosing soft curves in the furnishings; aligning sympathetic materiality, such as the black, steel-framed, bi-fold garden doors; and replicating the pale hues of the older part of the home into the new space.

The house now comprises four bedrooms, four bathrooms, an internal courtyard, a rear courtyard and a roof deck. "I love how much the home reflects our beautiful clients' personalities," says Jillian. "Every room speaks to their taste in a classic and timeless aesthetic, and the little pops of drama within the bathrooms and children's rooms additionally express their individuality."

The home's colour palette was centred around a muted blue favoured by the homeowners. "From there, we played with deeper navy tones, warm pinks, browns and nudes, teamed with silvers and greys, to create a cohesive and soothing atmosphere," says Jillian. For this reason, the living room walls of the original house were painted in warm greys that are tonally but comfortingly dim.

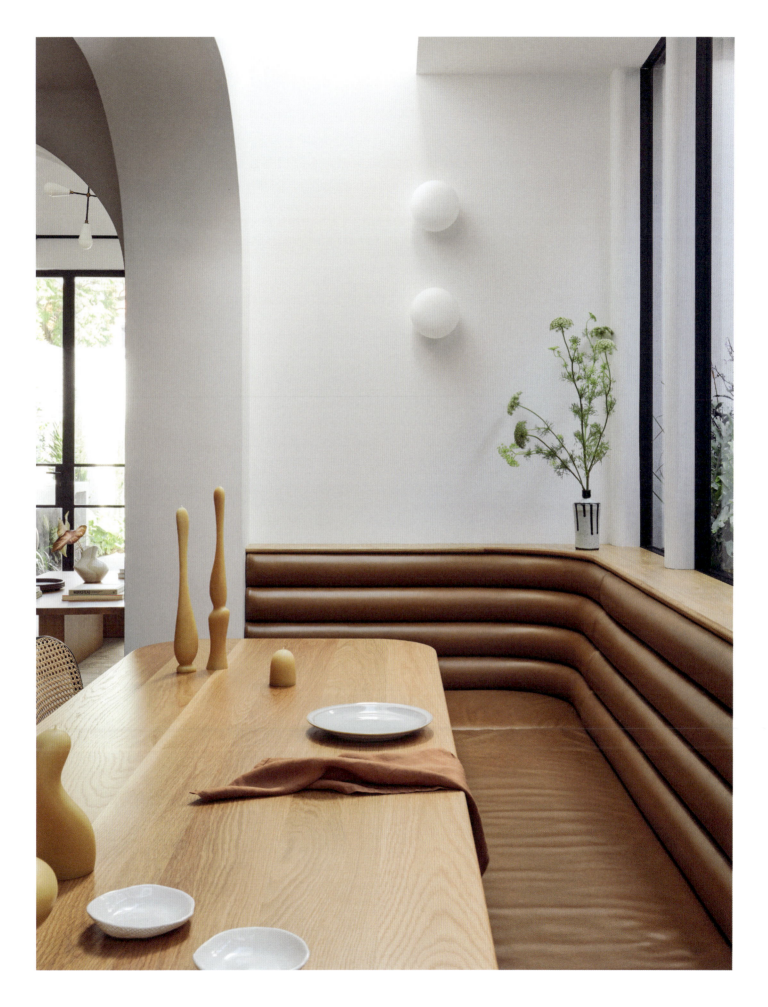

By contrast, the corridor then opens into a spacious and light-filled kitchen, dining and family room, with sunlight streaming through glass bi-fold doors at the rear of the home. This new extension replaces a demolished, unsalvageable lean-to that once housed a cramped kitchen, allowing the designer to create a space that is functional and aesthetically pleasing.

The use of specific materials also played a significant role in achieving complexity and contrast. Jillian highlights the ground-floor powder room as a favourite. "The steel-and-veneer floating adjacent to an Apparatus Triad sconce is very special. I also love the way the floating marble vanity is illuminated by a floor-to-ceiling fluted glass window, offering green glimpses of the internal courtyard beyond." In the kitchen, dark-grey Grigio San Marco marble for the island, benchtops and splashback; brass tapware and lighting; and ash-brown, wood-veneer joinery hit a striking note.

Adjacent to the kitchen, the dining area was compromised by a lack of space, so Jillian installed a custom banquette bench seat padded in leather to create a neat nook. The banquette's curvy shape is mimicked in the flat archway that connects the kitchen and dining zone to the casual living space and to the curved bench seating in the courtyard.

For furniture selection, Jillian focused on pieces with interesting details and curvaceous forms to enhance comfort and elicit delight. "You can see this in the curve of the arm of the Lola sofa by Jardan and the shape of the aptly named Bold Armchair by HC28 in the sitting room," she says. "It's also apparent in the custom pieces we created, such as the banquette and table in the dining area, and the upholstered bedhead and an elongated timber dresser for the primary suite."

Upstairs, the primary bedroom has French doors opening to a street-facing balcony and is characterised by soothing hues and period features, including the original fireplace in the adjacent marble-tiled bathroom.

Also on this floor is one of the children's rooms, where Jillian created delight with pretty wallpaper, wainscoting and antique furniture. She added a small ensuite featuring pink tiles and a rose marble vanity top. On the second floor, there are two more children's rooms that have tonal accents of blue, grey and tan. A study with city views is housed in the attic space on the third floor.

Through contemplative and curated interior design, Jillian has transformed Toxteth Terrace into a restful sanctuary exuding modernity and comfort and perfectly tailored to the needs of daily life. "I believe there is a calm and comforting essence to the idea of home and that the interior design should envelop, support and nurture its inhabitants. For me, this concept radiates from every corner of this historic Sydney home," says Jillian.

THE HOMES AND THEIR DESIGNERS

ART HOUSE (PP8–19)

Design studio: Chelsea Hing | chelseahing.com.au
Designer: Chelsea Hing
Portrait photo: Rhiannon Taylor

BELGRAVIA TOWNHOUSE (PP20–33)

Design studio: State of Craft | stateofcraft.com
Designer: Daniel Goldberg
Portrait photo: Milad Khatib
Architecture: Pringle Richards Sharratt Architects

BRAHEGATAN APARTMENT (PP34–43)

Design studio: Liljencrantz Design | liljencrantzdesign.com
Designer: Louise Liljencrantz
Portrait photo: Erik Lefvander

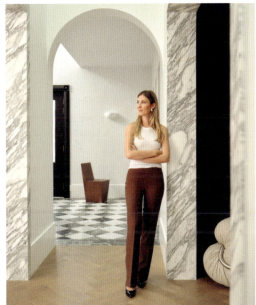

CARLOTTA TAKE TWO RESIDENCE (PP44–59)

Design studio: Esoteriko | esoteriko.org
Designer: Anna Trefely
Portrait photo: Dave Wheeler

LIGHT HOUSE (PP60–75)

Design studio: Smac Studio | smacstudio.com.au
Designer: Shona McElroy
Portrait photo: Dave Wheeler

MARYLEBONE PIED-À-TERRE (PP76–89)

Design studio: Maddux Creative | madduxcreative.com
Designers: Scott Maddux and Jo leGleud
Portrait photo: Ruth Ward

MATCHPOINT HOUSE (PP90–105)
Design studio: Duet | weareduet.com.au
Designers: Dominique Brammah and Shannon Shlom
Portrait photo: Anson Smart
Editorial stylist: Megan Morton

MOORE PARK RESIDENCE (PP106–121)
Design studio: EM Design Studio | emdesign.ca
Designer: Elizabeth Metcalfe
Portrait photo: Erin Leydon

NAPA VALLEY HOUSE (PP122–141)
Design studio: K Interiors | kinteriors.com
Designer: Kristen Peña
Portrait photo: Luis Peña

NEW SCHOOL RESIDENCE (PP142–155)
Design studio: Avenue Design Studio | avenue-designstudio.com
Designer: Holly Marder
Portrait photo: Alba Bruynel

PACIFIC PALISADES RESIDENCE (PP156–173)
Design studio: DISC Interiors | discinteriors.com
Designers: David John Dick and Krista Schrock
Portrait photo: Sam Frost

PLACE DAUPHINE PIED-À-TERRE (PP174–187)
Design studio: After Bach Studio | afterbach.com
Designer: Francesco Balzano
Portrait photo: Adel Slimane Fecih

QUEEN'S PARK TERRACE (PP188–201)
Design studio: Studio Skey | studioskey.com
Designers: Sophie Scott and Georgina Key
Portrait photo: Taran Wilkhu

SHADY CANYON RESIDENCE (PP202–219)
Design studio: Huma Sulaiman Design | humasulaiman.com
Designer: Huma Sulaiman
Portrait photo: Heather Gildroy

STATE STREET TOWNHOUSE (PP220–237)
Design studio: Frederick Tang Architecture | fredericktang.com
Designers: Frederick Tang and Barbara Reyes
Portrait photo: Gieves Anderson

STOCKHOLM RESIDENCE (PP238–251)
Design studio: AO/JN Interiors | aojninteriors.com
Designers: Jesper Nyborg and Alexandra Ogonowski
Portrait photo: Kristofer Johnsson

SUBDUED SOPHISTICATION CONDOMINIUM (PP252–265)
Design studio: Nunu Interior Design | nunuinterior.design
Designers: Chantal Philippe, with Elyssa Myers
Portrait photo: Alana de Haan

TOXTETH TERRACE (PP266–281)
Design studio: Jillian Dinkel | jilliandinkel.com
Designer: Jillian Dinkel
Portrait photo: Dave Wheeler
Architecture: Troy Newman
Stylist: Madeline McFarlane

ABOUT THE AUTHOR

Susan Redman is an Australian journalist, editor and stylist with a passion for architecture and design. This has led to a notable career writing about homes and the people who design, decorate and live in them. She is currently the Homes Editor for *Sunday Life*, a Fairfax Media lifestyle magazine.

Previously, Susan has worked as a design columnist for *The Sydney Morning Herald*, *The Age*, *Vogue Australia* and *The Japan Times*, and has been a regular contributor to various home and design publications, including *Vogue Living*, *Country Style*, *Home Beautiful*, *Belle*, *Gardening Australia*, *Black + White*, Houzz and Domain. She's also written extensively about fashion, art and travel.

In addition to *Curated Living*, Susan's other books are *Modern Houses in Black*, a title that explores the trend in black home design through a select collection of distinctive residential properties around the world; *Love Shacks*, a volume that not only features beautiful hideaways and retreats across the globe, but seeks to understand how people and places influence holiday home design; and *My Dream Kombi*, a book celebrating the retro design icon and the fascinating stories of the surfies, hippies and celebrities who travelled in them.

Published in Australia in 2025 by
The Images Publishing Group Pty Ltd
ABN 89 059 734 431

Offices

MELBOURNE	NEW YORK	SHANGHAI
Waterman Business Centre	6 West 18th Street 4B	6F, Building C, 838 Guangji Road
Suite 64, Level 2 UL40	New York, NY 10011	Hongkou District, Shanghai 200434
1341 Dandenong Road	United States	China
Chadstone, Victoria 3148	Tel: +1 212 645 1111	Tel: +86 021 31260822
Australia		
Tel: +61 3 8564 8122		

books@imagespublishing.com
www.imagespublishing.com

Copyright © Susan Redman and the photographers as indicated 2025
The Images Publishing Group Reference Number: 1692

All photography is attributed on the chapter title pages and in the Credits on pages 283–85, unless otherwise noted.
Page 2: Shade Degges (Huma Sulaiman Design, Shady Canyon Residence); page 4: Dave Wheeler (Smac Studio, Light House); page 6: Sam Frost (DISC Interiors, Pacific Palisades Residence); page 287: Mark Ryan (photograph of author).

All rights reserved. Apart from any fair dealing for the purposes of private study, research, criticism or review as permitted under the Copyright Act, no part of this publication may be reproduced, stored in a retrieval system or transmitted in any form by any means, electronic, mechanical, photocopying, recording or otherwise, without the written permission of the publisher.

 A catalogue record for this book is available from the National Library of Australia

Title: Curated Living: Elegant Interiors and Artful Homes
Author: Susan Redman
ISBN: 9781864709674

This title was commissioned in IMAGES' Melbourne office and produced as follows:
Editorial concept Susan Redman; *Art direction* Nicole Boehringer; *Editorial* Rebecca Gross, Helen Koehne, Jeanette Wall; *Production* Simon Walsh, Heather Johnson; *Prepress* A & S Graphics (Singapore).

EU GPSR Authorised Representative: Easy Access System Europe Oü
Company Registration ID: 16879218 | Address: Mustamäe tee 50, 10621 Tallinn, Estonia
Email: gpsr@easproject.com | Tel: +358 40 500 3575

Printed on 140gsm Hao Cai Woodfree FSC paper in China by C&C Offset Printing Co., Ltd.

IMAGES has included on its website a page for special notices in relation to this and its other publications.
Please visit www.imagespublishing.com

Every effort has been made to trace the original source of copyright material contained in this book.
The publishers would be pleased to hear from copyright holders to rectify any errors or omissions.
The information and illustrations in this publication have been prepared and supplied by the author and the contributors.
While all reasonable efforts have been made to ensure accuracy, the publishers do not, under any circumstances, accept responsibility for errors, omissions and representations, express or implied.